"The goal of education is not the mastery of subject matter but of one's person."

—David Orr

Thanks for sending me your new book. After I opened it, I couldn't stop and savored it in one sitting! It is superb. I've been waiting for this design book during five decades of work on transforming education from "child factories" to places of community, dignity, meaning and learning. I was delighted and astonished to find authors who captured the central elements of brain-compatible learning for the physical setting. I say, "Get, devour and apply this straightforward and beautifully illustrated guide to your learning setting."

> — Dr. Wayne Jennings, Director
> The Institute for Learning and Teaching,
> St. Paul, Minnesota

This is not only a book but a wonderful invitation to think about existing and future schools, and to share ideas. Sensitive to the needs and opportunities inherent in the notion of community and true to their Design Pattern #2, the authors have provided a "Welcoming Entry" to school design. They suggest a common language, refreshingly free of architectural or educational jargon, with underlying "nourishing patterns" and great respect for the changes in educational philosophy, which have brought us from the cells-and-bells model to holistic learning environments supporting creativity and innovation. The book is beautifully structured and illustrated with examples, as transparent as Design Pattern #9 wishes our schools to be. Both reassuring and stimulating, Prakash Nair, Randall Fielding and Jeff Lackney should be read not only by people planning new schools but by everyone, students included, who wish to make positive changes to their existing place of learning. Campfires, Waterholes and Caves could be created everywhere, and much else besides.

> — Dr. Walther Hetzer, Director
> St. Gilgen International School, Austria

It's an insanely good book. You also get high marks for the layout—clean, easy to read, compelling photos, helpful diagrams. It's actually a page-turner—not easy to do outside the fiction genre! You don't let the grass grow under your feet do you?! I plan to order a copy and know several others who will want one. Go guys, go.

> — Eeva Reeder, Curriculum/Instructional Coach,
> Nationally Recognized Teacher & Project Based
> Learning Expert, Seattle, Washington

With this book the authors continue the generous project they first commenced online with Designshare.com, providing insight and encouragement that will empower students, teachers, parents and educational administrators to actively participate in the creation of more effective learning environments.

> — Peter Jamieson, Faculty Developer
> University of Queensland, Australia

I am very excited about your new book. It will be extremely helpful to me. The most important element in planning is to recognize the need to consider what is a 21st Century school and how its educational program relates now and in the future to the school building. But educators and architects simply do not understand the concept and cannot think spatially.

Educators may appreciate that their programs would be more effective using different teaching techniques but they have trouble relating the concept to the building design. Architects often have no experience designing schools that reflect the newer approaches to teaching. Your book is the tool we need to explain how a good 21st century educational program relates to school building design. I know I will be recommending it frequently.

> — Joan Ponessa, Director of Research
> Education Law Center, New Jersey

Congratulations on the new book. I have enjoyed reading it on the bus on the way to work— I particularly like the use of sketches and photos to reinforce the message. One thing I was pleased with was consideration of the suitability of particular spaces for Multiple Intelligences— this is highly relevant but not something that is typically included. I also learned more about lighting from the book. I think it will be really useful in keeping all the interested parties in the school design process talking a common language.

> — Keith Lightbody, ICT Consultant
> Western Australia Department of Education,
> Perth, Western Australia

The Language of School Design: Design Patterns for 21st Century Schools provides a fresh and insightful look at how schools can be designed to facilitate children's learning and, equally important, teachers' teaching. It's a delightful book. Read it and you'll wish you had gone to a school built by its authors.

— William Brenner, Director
National Clearinghouse for Educational Facilities, Washington, D.C.

Designing a new school building should be an occasion when all kinds of people—architects, educators, parents, students, and community members—come together to re-create the school. Finally, there is an accessible visual vocabulary around which these important conversations can occur. Thank you!

— Barbara M. Diamond, Vice-president, Communities & School Facilities
Public Policy, KnowledgeWorks Foundation, Cincinnati, Ohio

A highly readable tome which also engages intellectually with its well thought-through concepts. This illustrative book is a must-have companion guide for all school planners who want to explore beyond the conventional in terms of the creative use of space. Indeed, everyone else in the educational field will also benefit from a reading.

— Wei Chuen, Ministry of Education, Singapore

I think this book will really stand out as a significant work through the way in which the clear connections between educational research and educational facility planning are made. You have listened to the needs of the two most important but sometimes forgotten groups— students and teachers— and taken the challenge to educational facility planners. By showing through case studies that good practice is all around us, you have taken notice of and given notice to some of the world's great school planning stories.

— Jeff Phillips, Client Services, Research & Development, Western Australia Department of Education

The Language of School Design is an outstanding resource for those interested in being a part of the conversations needed to design schools that will stand the test of time. The authors think about schools the way educators think about children— each as individual, and requiring unique, thoughtful solutions for diverse needs. The authors demonstrate a generous spirit of collaboration by inviting the reader into a visual conversation that seeks to understand deeper values about the design of schools. Through this publication, I believe they are entirely successful in their stated goal— to serve as a catalyst for creative thinking that benefits schools not yet developed. The writing is accessible; the format is lively, creative, and full of possibilities. Nair and Fielding have created a marvelous structure for an ongoing exchange that inspires us, organizes our thinking, and expands our vision of the possibilities of school design.

— Elizabeth A. Hebert, Ph.D., Principal
Crow Island School, 1112 Willow Road, Winnetka, Illinois

I am in awe of your ideas! Really, reading your book made me wish I had become an architect. Your ability to take complex thoughts and present them in a way which changes the paradigm and is understandable to the layman is nothing short of extraordinary. You show conclusively that it is possible to design schools in a way that will lead to increased student learning and improved faculty productivity. Any teacher would want to teach in your schools; any student would want to attend your schools! I recommend this book for anyone who is involved in making decisions about how schools should be designed and how classrooms can be structured. Whether building a new school, modifying an old building, or simply thinking about how furniture and displays can be most effective, this book is filled with inspirational ideas.

— Thomas R. Hoerr, Ph.D., Head of School, New City School, St. Louis, Missouri
Author, Becoming a Multiple Intelligences School (2000), ASCD

The Language of School Design has been an invaluable resource in aligning our instructional innovation agenda with the principles of school design for new school construction and facility refurbishment."

— Don Hoium, Director of Education, Regina Public Schools, Regina, Saskatchewan, Canada

Endorsed by the National Clearinghouse for Educational Facilities and KnowledgeWorks Foundation

The Language of School Design:
Design Patterns for 21st Century Schools

Prakash Nair   Randall Fielding   Jeffery Lackney

DESIGNSHARE.COM

THE LANGUAGE OF SCHOOL DESIGN: Design Patterns for 21st Century Schools

$45/Architecture/Education/School Reform
Copyright © 2005 – 2013
Printed In USA
First Edition 2005. Second Edition 2009. This Revised Edition Printed 2013.
DesignShare.com, Prakash Nair, Randall Fielding, Jeffery Lackney
ISBN 0-9762670-0-4

Endorsed by:
National Clearinghouse for Educational Facilities
The KnowledgeWorks Foundation

Front Cover Photo: *The "Plaza" at the Anne Frank Inspire Academy in San Antonio, Texas. Master Planner and Design Architect – Fielding Nair International.*

Back Cover Photo: *Main Entrance to the Douglas Park Elementary School, Regina, Canada. Master Planner and Design Architect: Fielding Nair International.*

Cover and Book Layout Design: *Union Design & Photo, www.uniondesignphoto.com.*

Table of Contents

Acknowledgements

To Jeff Lackney, our brother who left this world much too soon. Wherever you are, Jeff, know that you will always influence who we are as professionals and as people.

We would like to thank everyone who gave us their feedback on early drafts, guidance and constructive criticism. We hope you will see that we have listened to all of you! We are especially grateful to our expanding FNI family – you are each special and we would not be where we are without your passionate support and creative brilliance.

Our first editor Susan Meisel deserves special mention for suggesting the book's final title, *The Language of School Design*.

We would like to thank Catherine Roberts-Martin for her help in editing this third edition of the book as well as her time in directing Designshare.

Annalise Gehling has rewritten many sections of this book and developed a number of additions. She has also provided many great photos for the new version of the book, for which we are extremely grateful.

Deepti Nair has rewritten the "Dispersed Technology" chapter with Annalise. She also researched and wrote the "Home-like Bathrooms" chapter and developed the associated graphic pattern. She deserves kudos for her work.

Pamela Sampson, a professional journalist and editor, proofread the latest edition of this work.

Jeff and Kristin Stevens from Union Design & Photo, you know why we are thanking you. You guys were just great all the way as the designers of this book and we appreciate the special care and attention you gave to this project.

It is said that planners and architects can only be as good as their clients will let them be. Without question, the clients that made the projects in this book possible deserve credit for their courage to do the right thing—often against great opposition to their ideas. And so we thank all the clients representing the various projects used in this book to reference the design patterns and principles.

This book represents our attempt to put into writing years of learning about schools and school facilities from many people and many sources. But it is hard to separate who we are as professionals from the people we are as human beings. And so, the many people who helped us along the way to get us where we are today need thanking. Ultimately, it is their love, their encouragement and their wisdom that inhabit these pages.

The following acknowledgements are from Prakash:

To my mother and father for a lifetime of love—without you, there would be no one to thank; to Jody for your constant love, your wisdom, your support and your faith in me; to Deepti, whose loving, creative, independent spirit gave me the courage to pursue my own dreams; to Mallika for being wise far beyond your years, for inspiring me and teaching me about love and friendship; to Jake for your boundless energy, and for the laughter and joy you bring to my life every day; to Vanitha for setting me on the right path in life, to Uma for your love, courage and quiet dignity; to Aunty, Lux, Rajan, Dolly, Shampak and Sunny for welcoming me into your home and hearts; to Deepak, for being my best friend, for letting me be your shadow for the first 18 years of my life and for the tennis; to Suma, Nilu, CGR uncle and aunty for being my second family; to my sister Pam for your friendship and my nephew Joshua; to my little sister Randy for your kindness and your wise counsel; to Shree, Indu and Omi for sharing your home every summer and for giving me the precious gift of reading; to Stu and Rose for 30 years of friendship; to my Australian mates John Mayfield, Andrew Gehling, Andrew Bunting, Tim Gourlay, Lyle Catlin and Jeff Phillips for being such great ambassadors for the Aussies; to Gayle, my tennis partner and dear friend for your sage advice and guidance in the spiritual domain.; to Mom for making me feel loved like a son; to my mentor Ed Kirkbride and lovely Carole Kirkbride for all that you have done for me professionally and personally; and last but certainly not the least, to my partner Randy for eighteen years of joy, adventure, and lasting friendship.

The following acknowledgements are from Randy:

To my wife Kristina, for 30 years of love—my constant in a changing world; to my daughters Kira and Jacqueline, for giving unending meaning and joy to my life; to my parents, Max and Wilma, for a life-time of support, and for nurturing wisdom and creativity; to my brother Glen, for honesty and integrity; to Bert, Gretchen, Steve, Beth, and Jill—for brotherhood and sisterhood; to my partner Prakash—for his courage, vision and the gift of friendship; for the DesignShare community, the planning and design team at Fielding Nair International, our clients, and the students and professionals at the schools that we have touched—you have all served as my mentors.

The following acknowledgements are from Jeff:

I have a special place in my heart for my humble mentor of 25 years, Jerry Weisman of the University of Wisconsin-Milwaukee. His encouragement has greatly structured my thinking that lead to my most recent applied research in design patterns for schools. Running into Randy Fielding and Prakash Nair years later, I became quite excited to be a part of a new model of a school design practice that was forming in our heads, hearts and hands. Finally! A chance to design for the way learning happens within the context of good school design. We owe a deep debt of gratitude to Edward Kirkbride, CEFPI Planner of the Year, in bringing not only us together, but many others that have contributed to our field. I am so grateful for Anne Taylor, Director of the Environmental Institute at the University of New Mexico. As Jerry Weisman is my intellectual father, Anne Taylor is my intellectual mother. Her work is seminal to all the work I have been doing since I started thinking about learning environments. Finally, I must acknowledge Henry Sanoff, Professor Emeritus, North Carolina State University, for his tireless work to encourage the use of research and authentic collaboration among stakeholders in planning of schools that any good architect uses today. But I save my most heartfelt acknowledgements for my wife Jill, of over 15 years, who has been beside me all the way, through my crazy ideas, and continual health challenges; I know no human being to be as emotionally strong, a supportive friend, angel, helper, and partner. I have the deepest, most profound love for my son, Nick, who throws all his passion into that greatest of American pastimes, baseball. His total commitment to his passion as a young boy is one of my greatest joys and inspiration to move on. I am embarrassed to say I have learned more from my son than I have from anyone in the past 12 years. Finally, acting as guides (and at times jesters), this particular journey begins and ends with my father Robert R. Lackney AIA, and my mother Barbara Lackney, along with my brothers Todd, Christopher and Matthew.

The subject of this book—new educational environments for different ways of learning—has some parallels with how this book was created. How do two people write a book together?

Interestingly, this is not a question we ever asked when the first edition of this book was being created even though one of us (Prakash) lived in New York and now in Tampa, and the other (Randy) lives in Minneapolis. After all, if we can work together as business partners depending mostly on email, our Web site (for large downloads of electronic documents), the telephone and the occasional face-to-face meeting, usually at conferences or when we are out servicing one of our projects, surely we could do a book together.

Well, this product is proof that not only can two people from distant areas produce something together, but also that the new global order is fully upon us. When Randy first proposed the idea for this book and developed some of the first patterns, he was already on his way to Singapore and Australia to present these new concepts to communities in those countries. We continued to develop the book during Randy's trip, which coincided with Prakash's travels to the UK, India and Dubai. We also relied upon the work of our international partners and colleagues to guide us in this venture. In a very real way, this book is also a global effort because we have relied on many projects outside the USA to illustrate our ideas. As owners of DesignShare.com, we are fortunate to have access to over 500 school designs from 25 countries and we dipped into that treasure trove of ideas as we sat down to write this book. Almost any "expert" book on any topic today is bound to have a limited shelf life. You don't see too many software manuals anymore do you? That's because all the "updates" can make the manual obsolete before the shrink-wrap comes off. And so what we are trying to create is a classic "ideas book," built on some timeless principles, structured to lend itself to almost unlimited development and expansion.

When we got ready to produce this second edition of the book, we decided to bring in our "Third Musketeer" Jeff Lackney who has contributed a significant body of work to the education design profession. As third author, Jeff has developed the new patterns *Teachers as Professionals* and *Shared Learning Resources*. He has also redrawn the *Casual Eating* and *Flexibility, Adaptability and Variety* patterns. In addition, he provided the *Home as Template for School* section that has been added to the *Welcoming Entry* pattern. Some of Jeff's drawings are included in the book such as the Cayman Islands Small Learning Community in the first chapter. Jeff also served as a member of the design team on several schools featured in this book such as Sinarmas World Academy, Duke School, Cristo Rey High School and Scotch Oakburn College. Jeff passed away soon after the second edition of this book was published but his imprint remains strong in this Third Edition of the book. We are grateful that *The Language of School Design* preserves his important legacy as one of the foremost thinkers of our time.

Much of the new, creative material in this book has been added by Annalise Gehling, many significant edits were done by Clare Friedrich who also served as the project manager on this complex venture, and a new chapter on "Home-like Bathrooms" was written by Deepti Nair who also helped edit the completely rewritten "Dispersed Technology" chapter.

We are gratified that several respected people have endorsed this book. We also hope that practitioners of school planning and design, plus everyone involved with schools can take something useful away from this book. Our "field" goes beyond buildings to include education and community development as well. We are also optimistic that this book will serve as a catalyst for creative thinking that benefits schools being developed today and those to be developed tomorrow.

It is important for us to state what may be obvious to anyone who reads this book. We have a certain "viewpoint"—some might say "bias." We believe in a new paradigm of education that is very different from the factory model still practiced so widely in this country and abroad. We are not alone in the perspective we present. In fact, we are in very good company. We can go back in time to the father of the progressive movement, John Dewey himself, plus many others who have all proposed a better and more caring way to educate our children: from Howard Gardner to Debra Meier, from Alfie Kohn to Linda Darling Hammond, from Ted Sizer and Eliot Levine to Peter Senge and Jonathan Kozol.

For all their influence, if one were measuring the success of the progressives by numbers alone, it might appear that their call has gone largely unheeded. One might even say that the current standards-based focus has set back some of the gains toward the development of a system of schools that is forward-looking and mindful of the very different world our children will inherit. But unlike the past where progressive education was dismissed as a fringe movement, there is today a great sense of urgency among many important constituents, such as parents and state governments, to change what has not worked before. That could mean the adoption of policies that put into practice what the *No Child Left Behind* law in the United States supports only in theory—that education must work for *all* children and not only for a privileged few. This philosophy of serving all children underlies much of what the progressive education movement is about. Service to all children in an environment that is conducive to real learning does not mean diluting the quality of education, making it less rigorous or dispensing with structure where it is needed, as many in the so-called back-to-basics movement claim.

In our own modest way, we too see ourselves as champions for a traditionally disenfranchised group—the students. By writing this book, we are saying that it is possible to go beyond paying lip service to children's needs. We want everyone in our profession to understand that it is our work more than our words that can demonstrate our care

about the places in which our children spend most of their waking hours.

But schools are not only for children anymore. They are also for adults. Lifelong learning is not just a catch phrase, but also often the passport to survival and to a better life. And if so, shouldn't the school buildings we design reflect these priorities? And shouldn't schools live up to their promise of helping to create a fair and egalitarian society by looking forward and not backward?

These thoughts raise the inevitable question—should we stop building schools? It is reasonable to ask if we are stretching the definition of school too far when we apply it to tomorrow's places of learning. It is not simply a matter of semantics. There are few words more loaded with meaning in our society than the word "school." Inevitably, it conjures up images of the familiar and maybe even influences how we go about creating our future learning places. But the familiar is not the future. The future may belong not to school but to a new kind of learning place— the "Community Learning Center." At least that is what we predict. We have tried to back up our prediction with a strong rationale based on actual trends that are already manifesting themselves in communities across the U.S. and the world. The possible disappearance of school in favor of the Community Learning Center is the subject of a concluding essay included in this book, *"Should We Stop Building Schools?"*

We would love to hear from you. Do write to us at:

Emails

Prakash@FieldingNair.com
Randy@FieldingNair.com

Websites

http://DesignShare.com
http://FieldingNair.com

Introduction

INSPIRED BY ALEXANDER

When Christopher Alexander wrote *A Pattern Language* more than 30 years ago, he approached architecture from a unique perspective. He looked at the real world of people plus the buildings and spaces they inhabited in order to understand the connections between the built environment and the human psyche. Focusing on architectural and landscape attributes that worked, on places that felt pleasant or were spiritually uplifting and to which people were attracted rather than turned off, Alexander was able to identify many spatial patterns that nourish the human communities they support.

Design Process

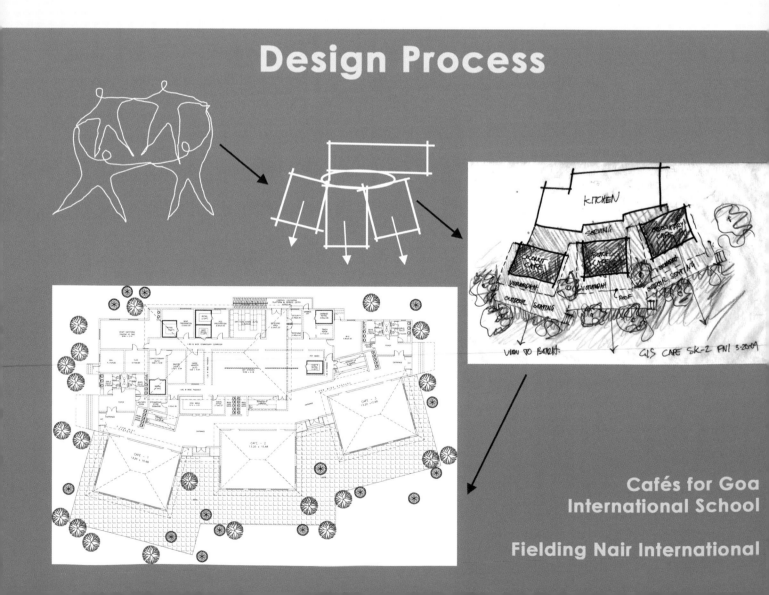

Cafés for Goa International School

Fielding Nair International

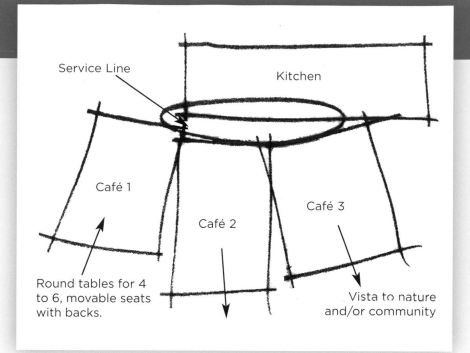

Service Line

Kitchen

Café 1

Café 2

Café 3

Round tables for 4 to 6, movable seats with backs.

Vista to nature and/or community

Figure i-1.
Diagrammatic pattern for cafés at Goa International School, India. Planner: Fielding Nair International (FNI); Architect: FNI with Dennis Coelho and Suhasini Ayer.

Figure i-2 (bottom left).
Illustrative pattern for Goa International School shows how the Design Pattern fits into the overall design process.

Interestingly, the larger body of architectural work, in the period immediately following the publication of Alexander's ground-breaking book, does not appear to have affected the way we build our homes, our towns and cities. However, over time, Alexander's work has gained credibility as the ideas he presented have begun to enter the scientific realm of complexity theory, fractals and neural networks—disciplines on the cutting edge of science. The "connections" between the built environment and healthy communities that Alexander was pointing out are now more readily apparent. Today, we know that human brains are actually hard-wired to understand and respond to patterns in all spheres of our life and, particularly, to those that exist within our built environments.

Our book, *The Language of School Design*, does not claim to be scientifically based. The book draws upon our own experience as school planners and the best practice of school design from over 20 countries, represented by hundreds of innovative school designs that we have published at DesignShare.com.

Why a Pattern Language for Schools?

We felt the need to develop a pattern language for schools for the simple reason that while Alexander's book is now beginning to influence the planning and design of healthy communities, transformation is painstakingly slow in the world of school design. Despite the fact that the educational establishment itself has embraced a number of innovative approaches over the years, architects often hear educators speak with a vocabulary reminiscent of their own childhood experiences in school buildings designed for a different time.

Why do schools look the way they do? Why is there a chasm between widely acknowledged best practice principles and the actual design of a majority of school facilities? Why has the connection between learning research and educational structures been so difficult to repair? These are the questions that we have been grappling with over the past decade as school planners.

A Common Design Vocabulary

From our own experience and from the research, we have begun to understand that one of the biggest roadblocks to innovation is the lack of a common design vocabulary that all school stakeholders can share. In other words, there is no quick and elegant fashion in which design ideas can be developed and tested in a way that truly involves all stakeholders.

Most of the larger school systems (and many smaller ones as well) rely on their own internal "quality control" methods to develop schools. But the inadvertent result of all this quality control is a lot of sameness and little innovation.

The climate in which schools are developed today, with heavy reliance on educational specifications, design guidelines, exemplars and prototypes, leaves little room for real creativity and innovation. Educational specifications create a school before it is created—design guidelines are too prescriptive (so that architects are often relegated to the role of assembling pieces instead of doing real design). Exemplars look good on paper or may have worked in certain specific circumstances, but have little to do with the needs of particular communities; and most prototypes are about cookie-cutter schools that don't even pretend to be community-specific. We firmly believe that schools need to grow from a shared vision. But we know that much can be lost in the translation of a written vision into built form. And so we need a graphic pattern language to supplement the written words—a pattern language that is so simple that every participant in the planning process can not only understand it, but actually create their own patterns or easily amend ones developed by their design professionals. In this sense, our pattern language differs from Alexander's in that we wanted to create an actual, usable design vocabulary for schools as a living, changing thing—similar to the spoken and written language that changes as cultures grow and change—but one that everybody can use.

29 Patterns Are Only A Beginning

We want to emphasize that we are not presenting these design patterns as a comprehensive vocabulary for school design. The 29 patterns contained here only *begin* to define the graphic language for the design of healthy and functional learning environments. To the extent possible, we have selected patterns that represent certain universal principles, though they are not to be used as a template or prototype of how any given element in a particular school should be designed.

School designers should look at these patterns as a starting point for developing their own patterns or modifying the ones provided here. Of course, in certain circumstances, some of these patterns will be usable without modification.

The professionals who reviewed this book submitted many useful suggestions that have already been incorporated into this revised second edition.

Two areas in particular have been explored and have considerably enriched the original patterns:

- Do the facilities created as a result of external educational forces such as state standards and required curricula help or hurt learning goals?

- How does the physical design of a school affect the social dynamics of the school community?

In the first edition we posed these two questions and we have had a chance to think about them during these past few years. Before reading our take on the issue, we encourage you to reflect on the extent to which this has been the case in your own communities. What were the expectations of the curriculum, and did they assume 'stand and deliver' pedagogy, or something more child-centered?

The environments of Reggio Emilia, Waldorf and Montessori schools, for instance, typically assume a child-centered pedagogy where teachers use a curriculum that focuses on the 'whole child' and acknowledges different learners' individual needs. Where there is an expectation of content-driven instruction in the curriculum, by contrast, the environment tends to reflect this by offering little in the way of comfort, stimulation or aesthetic beauty—things that might be considered surplus to the 'learning' requirements.

Some Pattern Ideas That Need to Be Further Developed

Things change. As we are writing, the Australian Government is busily conducting the first consultations on a new National Curriculum that will replace the State-based curricula currently in place. This will mean the second or third change in curriculum in five to ten years for most states. Since the two major parties are at war with each other over preferred pedagogies, and the party in power changes every few years, we could expect further significant change at least a second time within the next decade. Building to a curriculum seems folly when a building's lifetime will outlast 10 or more different mandated curriculum documents.

By only focusing on mandated curricula, we are far too narrow in our view of the scope of change affecting education. We are currently experiencing profound change in the manner in which we communicate with each other and disseminate information, which in turn has greatly altered the expectations of learners. We are also realizing, all too late, that our rates of consumption in the developed world are fast outstripping the rate at which the Earth's resources can be replenished and healed. What this means for what we teach and how it is learned has barely begun to be recognized.

Our humble suggestion in the face of this change is to create a range of opportunities for teachers to adapt their practice in response, and to honor as constant the ergonomic principles that relate to our development as human beings. In the "ergonomic" category we could direct you to the Patterns of *Daylighting, Natural Ventilation, Indoor–Outdoor Connection, Furniture: Soft Seating, Home-like Bathrooms* and *Designing for Multiple Intelligences*. We could also consider as 'ergonomic' the limit of 150 as a maximum number for *Small Learning Communities (SLCs)*, since beyond this size the nature of a community will change substantially and feelings of anonymity will increase exponentially.

'Opportunities' could be defined as any environmental feature, or lack thereof, that grants users the ability to change their environment to best meet their needs when engaged in a particular activity. Former Premier of Tasmania, Jim Bacon, remarked once that "schools should be places in which children and young people are granted opportunities to do/make/be/create or explore that are not available anywhere else in their lives." Using a commercial kitchen, a carpentry tool, a high-end piece of software, or a microscope, is a start. Meeting and working with older or younger peers is an opportunity many don't have in their home lives. Discussing big philosophical questions with each other and expert adults is another.

Then again, meetings and discussion can increasingly occur virtually, which brings us to our more bold suggestion—to look well beyond our current conception of 'schools'. Even SLC-based campuses, with outstanding physical attributes, are often 'islands for learning' with little more than token connections to the communities beyond. We are still looking at single-purpose institutional solutions that warehouse children, and whatever great opportunities we create on that campus still tend to be very inwardly focused.

That is why we are so keen to see our plans and designs for a Shared Community Facility in Regina, Saskatchewan become reality. This project has fully dispensed with the very idea of school as a box for learning and, instead, brings together a diverse group of stakeholders under one roof. Here, "learning" equals "living" and occurs naturally as the by-product of real-world transactions within a healthy community.

The second question posed in our earlier edition has continued to gain momentum and has reached the public eye at last. As globalization, economics, learning disabilities, class size and e-learning dominate education conversations, the question at hand remains as relevant as ever: *How does the physical design of a school affect the social dynamics of the school community?*

The physical environment, the social structure within which it is embedded and which it supports, as well as its symbolic meanings determine to a large extent the kinds of experiences children have and what they learn about the world. The content of development cannot be thought of separately from the structure of development. All of child development involves socialization.

We know from environment and behavior studies that the social needs of an individual refer to the desired amount of social interaction with others in a given space. A physical space can hinder learning either directly (for instance via noise or crowding), or symbolically (students make limiting assumptions about learning based on the limited way it is presented at school).

We can look at the issue of physical environment and its effect on social climate through two perspectives. The first is that of the teacher. Studies have found that the higher the quality of space in a school, the more likely the teachers were to be sensitive and friendly toward children, to encourage children in their self-chosen activities, and to teach consideration for oneself and others. The second perspective is that of the student. When a student attributes poor classroom design and maintenance to a lack of respect on the part of the institution, the social dynamics between peers and their teachers may shift negatively. On the contrary, when students feel cared for and respected, they are more likely to behave well and interact on more friendly terms with their peers and teachers.

Certain designs have been found to call for physical and social behaviors in children as well. For instance, studies show that high ceilings encourage very active behavior (such as a typical gymnasium), while low ceilings encourage quiet behavior (a small reading corner). Larger, more open spaces cause children to exhibit greater amounts of tactile and sensory exploration and greater direction of attention to other children. Likewise, they tend to offer more opportunities for rewarding child-to-child interaction and more opportunity for autonomy and initiative. Yet these same open spaces provide fewer opportunities for cognitive engagement. The environment clearly stimulates certain behaviors and affects levels of energy. To create a supportive school environment, the spaces in which children spend their days must be carefully planned, designed and built.

Diagrammatic and Illustrative Patterns

Each of the 29 patterns (and their sub-patterns) in this book can be categorized as either diagrammatic or illustrative.

Diagrammatic Patterns: A diagrammatic pattern is a rough sketch of a "big idea." In this sense, a diagrammatic pattern is somewhat generic and universal in scope. That doesn't mean a diagrammatic pattern will represent a spatial relationship that works in all cases, but it is intended to represent a particular philosophy of planning and design, more than the actual design of a particular school. See Figure i-1.

Diagrammatic patterns are useful early in the planning process as a graphic sounding board to gauge a client's general educational philosophy and design preferences. A diagrammatic pattern can also be created very quickly and on the fly to capture specific ideas during planning and community meetings. These kinds of early sketches often influence the final design.

Illustrative Patterns: Illustrative patterns are different from diagrammatic patterns in one important respect—they are more detailed. It is not unusual for an illustrative pattern to also be somewhat universal in scope. In general, the more detailed the illustration is, the less universal its scope. If this is so, why bother with an illustrative pattern and can it even qualify as a pattern? The answer is yes. We believe that any illustration can be a pattern as long as it documents spatial relationships in a way that communicates the big idea. That is why diagrammatic patterns intended to first introduce a big idea often turn into illustrative patterns to flesh out that big idea. In Figure i-2, the illustrative pattern shows how the design pattern fits into the overall design process.

How to Use the Pattern Language Method

Let us take a moment to introduce how exactly our Pattern Language Method can help in the design process by looking at a specific example of its use. Figure i-2 shows the stages in the development of a cafeteria design for a school that was aided by the use of design patterns. This client originally started with the idea of building a typical large school "cafeteria." During the course of the discussion utilizing the Pattern Language Method, we were able to understand how the cafeteria should not only reinforce the school's desire to create "community," but also give a special identity to each of its Small Learning Communities. We understood that this could not be done without somehow breaking down the scale of the large cafeteria into smaller cafés. However, because of financial constraints, we needed to service all the cafés utilizing one central kitchen.

These discussions led to a very rough penciled pattern showing how three separate cafés might be developed that could be serviced by one central kitchen (Figure i-1). Once the team agreed with this direction, a more illustrative pattern was developed by the planning team that allowed the architects to produce a scaled schematic design drawing (Figure i-2). Utilizing this system, we can break down the communication barriers to good design that often beset school architecture.

In Pattern #29: *Bringing It All Together*, we look at another example—this time for a whole school. This is to demonstrate how the Pattern Language Method we are proposing is not only about the elements that make up a school, but also about effectively setting up the design for a whole campus.

Knowing its value as an important aid in the school planner's toolbox, we are interested in continuously expanding our graphic "vocabulary" and sharing the information with all those involved in the creation of schools and school facilities.

With far less investment of money and effort than the traditional system, where designers and school stakeholders do not share a common language of school design, the Pattern Language Method can help build consensus quickly, and create superior designs.

It is clear that most school architecture tends to look at spaces in a linear way—that means we first decide what a space would be used for and then we design the space for that activity. This kind of thinking ignores the complexity and research about the human brain and human experience, resulting in the design of static spaces that inhibit learning.

The reality is that the design of learning environments is a complex assignment. While the solutions may be simple or elegant, they can almost never be simplistic. We need to understand the complexity of the human experience in order to understand what learning is about. We also need to recognize that it is almost impossible to solve a design problem unidimensionally. Everything we do as designers impacts the users of the space at many different levels.

What exactly in the whole range of human experiences does The Pattern Language Method encompass? In response, we can say that it deals with four major and simultaneous realms of human experience—spatial, psychological, physiological and behavioral. Each of these realms is characterized by multiple attributes. See Table i-1.

What is fascinating about this list is the obvious interconnectedness of the attributes across the four realms and the fact that the interconnectedness is nonlinear. That means it is nearly impossible to identify simple cause-and-effect relationships between specific attributes that would hold true always. These relationships are always contextual, but they are far from being outside our ability to control. For example, research tells us that as humans our sense of sight (physiological realm) is a major emotional (psychological realm) trigger. We also know that our emotions can elicit a physical response (behavioral realm) such as laughter when we are happy, facilitated to a greater or lesser degree by the environment (spatial realm).

Let us look, for example, at "Light on Two Sides" in the original *A Pattern Language* by Christopher Alexander, which advocates having daylight penetrate a room from more than one direction. The purpose is to reduce stark contrasts that characterize rooms with only one window. Of course, if the problem were simply one of lighting a given space, it could be accomplished with one window or even with adequate artificial light but that would miss Alexander's point, which goes to the heart of how we as humans experience our environment.

Going beyond individual patterns and focusing on how they work together, Alexander likes to refer to a building's functional complexity using such words as "dense" and "profound." He compares a well-designed building to poetry as opposed to prose, because the former can be understood at many different levels that go beyond the meaning of the individual words. In the same way, a good building can either string together patterns without any real coherence or assemble them to create poetry in design form.

This is the fundamental thesis behind the Pattern Language Method advocated by Alexander and by us in this book: that there are certain recognizable patterns that define healthy spatial relationships both at a micro and macro level. Unlike Alexander's ambitious work, which encompasses human environments at every scale, we have limited our focus to the design of learning environments. However, we acknowledge that the learning environment is actually nothing more than one piece of a larger pattern and that good planning requires that each piece be respectful of the overall patterns for communities and towns that the original *A Pattern Language* identifies. In this sense at least, it is really impossible to ignore the larger context in which a learning community is situated. We have addressed this in a limited way in Pattern #24, *Connected to the Community*, but we strongly urge our readers to read

Alexander's *A Pattern Language* for a treatise on the larger spatial patterns in our communities, towns and cities.

To pass the test and qualify as a "pattern," there has to be a certain universality to its application. A good example is Pattern #23, *Local Signature*, which cites three extremely diverse examples from Perth, Western Australia; Goa, India; and Bridgehampton, New York. Even though the examples themselves would seem to have nothing in common, the common human experience they seek to evoke ties them together within one pattern.

The Pattern Language Method is a sensible way to provide room for these various facets of our essential natures to be stimulated, while at the same time allowing for the wide range of human interests and behavioral tendencies to coexist peacefully. An example of how the four realms can be made to work in practice is the placement of an art room with natural lighting and a landscape view (physiological and spatial realms) intended to evoke a desired creative response (behavioral realm) by ensuring a suitable peaceful

and reflective frame of mind (psychological realm). The ability to rearrange the room so that different persons can organize themselves at different times of the day for different artistic activities makes the design more robust. Our desire for flexibility must not supersede our primary intent, which is to positively manage the complex relationship within the four realms in order to create an environment conducive to artistic endeavors.

It is also clear from the above discussion that there is a certain synergy within the patterns themselves—a point we touched upon earlier. The above example for the design of an art room borrows ideas from various patterns in the book: "Daylight and Solar Energy," "Indoor–Outdoor Connection," "Student Display Space," "Interior and Exterior Vistas," and "Music and Performance."

A school, or any learning environment for that matter, in its totality represents a very complex organization, but one that can usually also be represented in the form of a pattern. An example of this is "Bringing It All Together,"

Realms of Human Experience Within the Purview of School Planning and Design	Attributes
Spatial	Intimate, Open, Bright, Closed, Active, Quiet, Connected to nature, Monumental, Technological
Psychological	Soothing, Safe, Awe-inspiring, Joyful, Playful, Stimulating, Creative, Encouraging reflection, Spiritually uplifting, Creating a sense of community
Physiological	Warm, Cool, Cozy, Breezy, Healthy, Aromatic, Textured, Visually Pleasing
Behavioral	Independent study, Collaborative work, Teamwork, Physical fitness activity, Research, Writing, Reading, Computer work, Singing, Dancing, Performing, Presenting, Large group work, Communing with nature, Designing, Building, Teaching, Relaxing, Reflecting, Playing

Table i-1.
The four realms of human experience and their corresponding attributes.

Pattern #29. The larger pattern will only make sense, however, when its sub-groupings are also recognized as complete systems themselves, deserving to be represented as patterns.

While we are only listing the positive attributes of the four major realms of human experience, many attributes have a paired negative attribute as well, that we as school designers don't want to trigger via the design we create. Examples of negative attributes would be claustrophobic, stale, gloomy, drafty, dysfunctional, depressing, frightening, inflexible, uncomfortable, banal, and so on.

Obviously, the permutations and combinations by which the various positive attributes can come together are almost infinite, and that is why healthy patterns are important to identify. The patterns included in this book have been developed over time and are based upon our experience with spatial relationships that are functional at a very fundamental human level. These patterns respect the great complexity of human needs that vary not only with time and the context in which people operate, but also from person to person.

Beyond the curricula and tests that define so much of what school is all about, it is ultimately our ability to enrich the four realms of human experience noted above that will determine how well we have done our work as school planners, designers and as members of a learning community.

We have selected the 29 school design patterns in Table 2 because they represent a fairly complete range of the various design principles that define best practice. It is important to stress that dozens of variations of each diagram we have provided are possible. The number of diagrams that can be done is only limited by the school planning team's imagination. Yet each diagram included in this book embodies certain universal principles—and the principles themselves are less likely to change from site to site.

The 29 patterns and additional sub-patterns in this book have been ordered into six categories as follows:

1. Parts of the Whole
2. Spatial Quality
3. Brain-Based
4. High Performance
5. Community Connected
6. Higher Order

We talked earlier about interconnectedness of the four realms of human experience that healthy patterns try to balance. A great deal of interconnectedness of patterns also occurs across the six areas listed above as shown in Table i-2.

Individual patterns may themselves have qualities that qualify them for consideration under more than one category; however, we have tried to identify each pattern under the one category that describes its purpose most clearly. In only two cases have we placed a pattern under more than one category; and in these cases, we have identified the primary category under which each one belongs. (Pattern #1, "Principal Learning Areas," is primarily classified as category one, Parts of the Whole, but also fits the description of category six, Higher Order. Pattern #2, "Welcoming Entry," is primarily classified as category one, Parts of the Whole, but also fits the description of category five, Community Connected.)

We expect that all future patterns will fall into one of the above six categories though we are open to considering the inclusion of additional categories should we discover a school design pattern that does not fit the description of the above categories as follows:

Parts of the Whole

These are patterns that describe specific functional areas of a school. The first eight patterns presented in this book starting with *Principal Learning Areas* and ending with *Casual Eating Areas* and Pattern #25 (*Home-like Bathrooms*) look individually at several key parts of the whole school—thus the term "parts of the whole." However, not every school will contain all the parts we have discussed under Pattern Numbers 1 through 8 and 25. By the same token, it is possible that we have not listed every functional area that a school might contain. Many specialty academies contain highly customized spaces designed to meet particular functional needs. For example, the Center for Advanced Research and Technology (CART) in Clovis, California contains a Forensics Lab whose requirements may only be partially captured by the patterns in this book.

Spatial Quality

These are patterns that describe the quality of a given space or spaces and cut across functional areas. Transparency and flexibility, for example, are spatial qualities that apply to several of the other patterns.

Brain-Based

The primary facet of a brain-based pattern is that it responds to some particular aspect of brain-based research. Patterns in this category deal with the design of spaces that stimulate the brain in ways that are beneficial to learning and overall human development. The five patterns listed under this category are important to consider in the design of any and all parts of the school and relate again to the concept of interconnectedness.

High Performance

High Performance is a term that applies to the efficient operation of the building, as well as the way in which it is designed to get the best performance from its occupants by providing a healthy, safe and cheerful environment. These are patterns that highlight a building's connection with nature, its sustainable qualities, and the opportunities that are available to translate the way it is put together into self-evident learning tools—thus the term, "3-D Textbook."

Community Connected

There is ample evidence that schools that are integral parts of their communities work better. Not only are students of community schools more likely to get a better education, but community schools also serve to strengthen social ties and build economic value for the neighborhood as a whole. But Community Connections as a pattern goes beyond making schools into community icons; it involves locating the school in a place that allows the students to get at least a part of their education by participating in activities within the community and outside the school building. A school can thus be "connected" to the community by having students take part in community service assignments, by working at local businesses, corporations and institutions, and by utilizing the resources of existing community facilities such as the local YMCA or library.

Higher Order

We define a Higher Order pattern as one that encompasses other patterns within it. The most obvious examples of these are Pattern #28, *Safety and Security* and Pattern #29, *Bringing It All Together*. These are patterns that show how an entire school might be arranged and, therefore, includes various components that can themselves be represented as patterns. At a smaller scale, Pattern #1 also qualifies as a Higher Order Pattern because its sub-patterns are actually combinations of simpler concepts that are put together using stand-alone elements like the Learning Studio and the Advisory.

Table i-2 (right). Classification of patterns.
Please note that Patterns 25, 26 and 27 were added to the revised second edition of the book which explains why they do not appear in the list to the right and within the book itself adjacent to the other patterns in their category. Doing so would have required the renumbering of the patterns from the original book which we chose not to do. The only pattern whose number does not match that of the first edition is *Bringing it All Together* which we felt should remain as the last pattern in the book.

Pattern #	Description	Parts of the Whole	Spatial Quality	Brain-Based	High Performance	Community Connected	Higher Order
					Pattern Type		
1	Principal Learning Areas — Classrooms, Learning Studios, Advisories and Small Learning Communities	**X**					X
2	Welcoming Entry — Home as a Template for School	**X**				X	
3	Student Display Space	X					
4	Home Base and Individual Storage	X					
5	Science Labs, Art Studios and Life Skills Areas	X					
6	Music and Performance	X					
7	Health and Physical Fitness	X					
8	Casual Eating Areas	X					
9	Transparency and Passive Supervision		X				
10	Interior and Exterior Vistas		X				
11	Dispersed Technology		X				
12	Indoor/Outdoor Connection		X				
13	Furniture: Soft Seating		X				
14	Flexibility, Adaptability and Variety		X				
15	Campfire Space			X			
16	Watering Hole Space			X			
17	Cave Space			X			
18	Designing for Multiple Intelligences			X			
19	Daylight and Solar Energy				X		
20	Natural Ventilation				X		
21	Learning, Lighting and Color				X		
22	Sustainable Elements and Building as 3-D Textbook				X		
23	Local Signature					X	
24	Connected to the Community					X	
25	Home-like Bathrooms	X					
26	Teachers as Professionals		X				
27	Shared Learning Resources			X			
28	Safety and Security		X			X	**X**
29	Bringing It All Together						**X**

* Where a Pattern is listed under more than one category, then the bold-faced "X" indicates that pattern's primary classification.

No book about school design would be complete without a discussion of the "classroom" and what this space might look like in tomorrow's school. In fact, it is legitimate to ask if the classroom should continue to reign as the primary building block of a school as it undoubtedly does today.

Cristo Rey High School in Minneapolis, MN (pictured below) is broken down into four Small Learning Communities of 125 students each. Planner and Design Architect: Fielding Nair International.

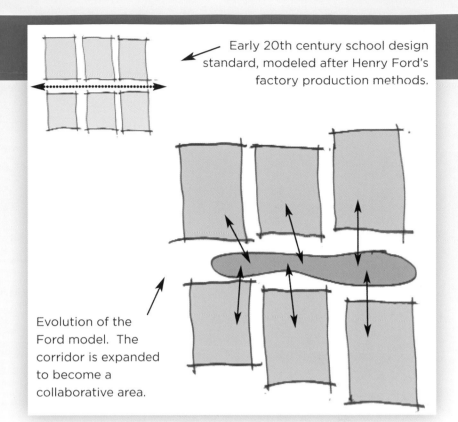

Early 20th century school design standard, modeled after Henry Ford's factory production methods.

Evolution of the Ford model. The corridor is expanded to become a collaborative area.

Figure 1-1.
Design Patterns #1 and #1a: Traditional Plan and Ford Model Evolution.

Cells-and-Bells (Ford) Model

Before we can talk about design, it is valuable to take another look at what the classroom represents. The classroom is the most visible symbol of an educational philosophy. It is a philosophy that starts with the assumption that a predetermined number of students will all learn the same thing at the same time from the same person in the same way in the same place for several hours each day.

A classroom's simplistic design also assumes that the significant part of a student's learning occurs in the transmission of knowledge from the teacher to the student in a somewhat linear fashion. A 750 square-foot space with 25 student armchair-tablet desks and a teacher's desk at the front of the room makes eminent sense if this is, indeed, what learning is all about. And how are those four computers sitting in the back of the room being used? They become additional learning resources, like textbooks, but do not change the essential model of the teacher firmly in command of the students under her supervision and active tutelage.

Why is it called the Ford Model?

Under the original classroom-based model of a school, it made sense to regiment several classrooms next to each other and place them on long corridors that could be easily supervised. This was efficient from the standpoint of space and provided the adults with the most "control," since students leaving classrooms had nowhere to go but into the easily-supervised corridors from where they could move to the other learning spaces like science labs and art rooms—also preferably set up along a double-loaded corridor.

The classroom model worked best from a control standpoint if the day itself could be broken down into neat little segments (45 minutes being the preferred period after which one activity would shut down and another would begin) and if the segmentation could be announced by bells that, over time, literally programmed the students to switch gears on command. Thus the term "cells and bells" was born. The vast majority of school buildings are in fact cells-and-bells models. For illustrative purposes only (in other words, we are not suggesting that this is a workable model for 21st century schools), we start, therefore, with Pattern # 1—the early 20th century cells-and-bells pattern in which several regularly shaped classrooms are aligned along a double-loaded corridor.

One way of looking at the traditional classroom model is to equate it to a factory or production model in which the philosophy of the assembly line with its inherent efficiencies dictates the look and feel of the school. The assumption of such a design is that students are empty vessels to be filled with knowledge, like widgets on a conveyor belt, proceeding along a production line over the course of years (in the case of elementary schools) or day after day (in the case of secondary schools). Hence the 'Ford Model' name.

> Under the new learning paradigm, we are looking at a model where different students (of varying ages) learn different things from different people in different places in different ways and at different times.

One of the defining features of the Ford Model, in whatever field it is applied to, is that the inputs are standard, and the outputs are standard. The Ford company, to begin with, made just one kind of car—the Model T. But that business model didn't last long. Diversification and then customization of factory-built products quickly became the new standard, as manufacturers realized that *the same products did not work for everyone.*

Around the same time as the Ford factory model was established and began to evolve, the school models we are so familiar with today also became established. But unlike the continually evolving, highly adaptable and purpose-built factories that quickly became sites for producing diverse products, school design stalled in the Ford era.

This was despite it being painfully clear that students were not identical widgets to be molded in identical ways for identical outcomes.

Assumptions of the Ford Model:

- All students are ready to learn the same thing at the same time in the same way from the same person.

- Learning is passive.

- One teacher can be all things (mentor, guide, lecturer, subject matter expert, caregiver) to 20-30 students simultaneously.

- Learning happens under teacher control.

Sadly, the assumptions of the Ford model have had teachers somewhat hamstrung without knowing it. Graduating teachers expect that they will be working in this isolated setting and that their practice will be somewhat private, at least from their colleagues. Differentiated instruction is always planned within a setting that is fundamentally opposed to the idea. In the next sections we will explore some patterns that, while operating within the more macro patterns of schools, curriculum and local communities, do support a more personalized learning paradigm.

Ford Model Evolution

This is the most basic step away from the Ford Model and while it requires no fundamental changes to teacher-centered teaching methodologies it does open up several new opportunities for personalized and student-directed, project-based learning. We can amend the plan somewhat to create an expanded corridor. See Figure 1-1. An expanded main central corridor can also satisfy the need for social learning, by slightly changing the dynamic of the control model and making the school design more progressive.

Done well, an expanded corridor could function as a 'Learning Street' though we have not seen any Ford Model

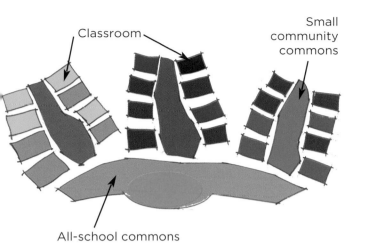

Classroom

Small community commons

All-school commons

Figure 1-2.
Design Pattern #1b : Finger Plan.

Evolution plans done well enough to qualify as Learning Streets. For a more complete discussion of Learning Streets, please see the discussion in the essay, "The Great Learning Street Debate," at the end of this book.

Another simple fix to the cells-and-bells model is the installation of operable walls between two classrooms on either side of the corridor. This allows greater flexibility in the way the overall space is utilized and also permits two teachers to collaborate and "team-teach."

Taking this one step further, some part of the corridor walls along the classrooms could be glazed to allow in natural daylight and also create "Transparency," which is another important design principle in new paradigm schools (see Design Pattern #9).

Taking the development of the double loaded model even further, sometimes referred to as the "finger plan," the pattern in Figure 1-2 shows smaller groupings of classrooms, six to eight at the most, pulled away from the main corridor. In this arrangement, the classroom cluster becomes a destination and not part of the larger thoroughfare. The finger plan has an added benefit in that it opens up the opportunity to make the main circulation spine into a Learning Street.

While it is a simple departure from the traditional corridor model, the finger plan model can have significant psychological benefits for students who are now better able to define their "Home Base" and thus take ownership of it. In order for these benefits to be fully realized, each cluster of rooms should be somehow differentiated from the remaining clusters so that it has its own unique identity. This can be accomplished by giving each wing a different architectural character, changing color schemes, providing different options for display of student work and so on. In the end, however, a classroom cluster within a simple finger plan may not qualify as a Small Learning Community because it lacks various common elements beyond classrooms that make each finger self-contained.

We will look later at concepts that take the finger plan to the next level in order to create Small Learning Communities or SLCs.

First, however, let us look at the reasons for departing from the traditional model of school and toward a new 21st century model. We now have abundant evidence from the frontiers of brain-based research that learning is not linear, but holistic, and that it is not unidimensional but multifaceted. As we move into the post-knowledge economy, we should be looking beyond the "knowledge worker" who is now a global commodity. <u>Our most valuable export as a country will be creativity and innovation and these skills are not developed in the cells-and-bells model of school.</u>

Under the new learning paradigm, we are looking at a model where different students (of varying ages) learn different things from different people in different places in different ways and at different times.

Clearly, it is hard to reconcile the old and new models of school. The spaces set up for the old paradigm would be extremely difficult to tailor so that they function well for the new model. To what extent such change may or may not be possible will vary from school building to school building and will depend upon how many of the following modalities of learning can be supported by the physical spaces. By looking at existing or proposed school designs with this list in mind, it will be easier to gauge their suitability to serve 21st Century learning needs.

Figure 1-3.
Exterior of L-shaped classrooms, Crow Island School in Winnetka IL. One of the first schools to feature the L-shaped Learning Studio. Architect: Perkins, Wheeler & Will, and Saarinen.

20 Learning Modalities

The 20 Learning Modalities (this may not be a complete list) that the physical school must support are[1]:

1. Independent study
2. Peer tutoring
3. Team collaboration
4. One-on-one learning with teacher
5. Lecture format — teacher-directed
6. Project-based learning
7. Technology with mobile computers
8. Distance learning
9. Internet-based Research
10. Student Presentation
11. Performance-based learning
12. Seminar-style instruction
13. Inter-disciplinary learning
14. Naturalist learning
15. Social/emotional/spiritual learning
16. Art-based learning
17. Storytelling
18. Design-based learning
19. Team teaching/learning
20. Play-based learning

A traditional cells-and-bells design will come up short against the above list because it is primarily set up for the lecture format. In Figures 1-1 and 1-2, we see that the traditional model can be pushed so that at least some of the new learning modalities can be accommodated.

This does not preclude the need to ask: Is the classroom obsolete? At some pure level, the answer to that question would be yes. But at a more practical level, we have to accept the reality that there are millions of classrooms already built in this country with thousands being added constantly.

[1] It is important to remember that these learning modalities do not all need to be supported under one roof since some schools may have auxiliary or community facilities that are brought into play to augment school facilities.

The Learning Studio

Given that the "classroom" itself will continue in some iteration into the foreseeable future, let us look at design patterns where the cells-and-bells model is amended so that the classroom goes from a rectangular box to a more flexible "Learning Studio." The term Learning Studio is sometimes used to refer to an L-shaped classroom which is, actually, not a new idea. One of the earliest schools featuring L-shaped classrooms configured like Learning Studios is the Crow Island School in Winnetka, Illinois built in 1940—Figure 1-3. Today, 65 years since its opening, the architecture of the Crow Island School remains relevant—more so even than many of the schools being built today. In his article, "The L-Shaped Classroom—A Pattern for Promoting Learning," Peter Lippman makes a strong connection between the shape of the classroom and its ability to function as a Learning Studio with multiple activity centers.

Figure 1-4 shows the characteristics of a Learning Studio and Figure 1-5 shows that two Learning Studios can be arranged to form a "Learning Suite." This is further described by two floor plans. The first illustrates one application of a Learning Studio. Figure 1-6 shows the plan for an Advanced Learning Module—which is a new generation of modular classrooms and schools able to meet temporary school needs. This irregular plan creates breakout spaces and flexible learning zones that support a significant number of the learning modalities from the above list. It supports small groups and individual students in pursuing a wide variety of activities.

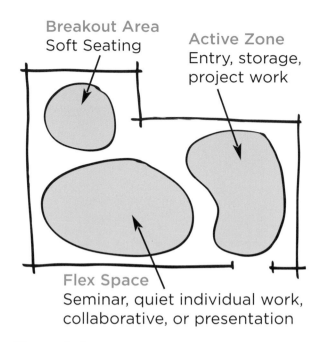

Figure 1-4.
Design Pattern #1c: Learning Studio.

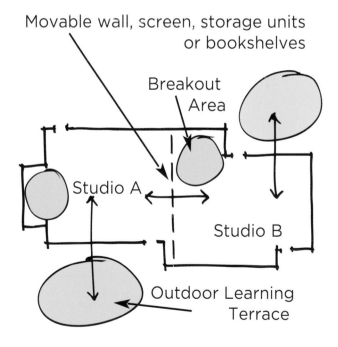

Figure 1-5.
Design Pattern #1d: Learning Suite. Each studio has its own entry, breakout area, and outdoor connection, and may operate as a single studio or combined with the adjacent studio into a learning suite.

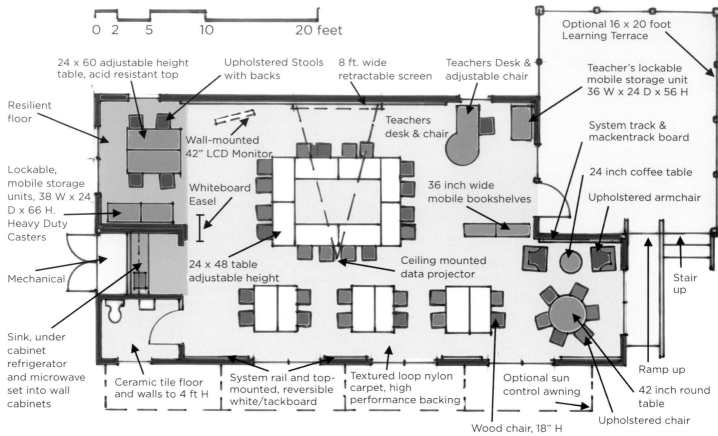

24 x 60 adjustable height table, acid resistant top

Upholstered Stools with backs

8 ft. wide retractable screen

Teachers Desk & adjustable chair

Optional 16 x 20 foot Learning Terrace

Resilient floor

Wall-mounted 42" LCD Monitor

Teachers desk & chair

Teacher's lockable mobile storage unit 36 W x 24 D x 56 H

System track & mackentrack board

Lockable, mobile storage units, 38 W x 24 D x 66 H. Heavy Duty Casters

Whiteboard Easel

36 inch wide mobile bookshelves

24 inch coffee table

Upholstered armchair

Mechanical

24 x 48 table adjustable height

Ceiling mounted data projector

Stair up

Sink, under cabinet refrigerator and microwave set into wall cabinets

Ceramic tile floor and walls to 4 ft H

System rail and top-mounted, reversible white/tackboard

Textured loop nylon carpet, high performance backing

Optional sun control awning

Ramp up

42 inch round table

Wood chair, 18" H

Upholstered chair

Figure 1-6.

Learning Studio-based design for Advanced Learning Environment Solutions, Inc. Planning and Design: Fielding Nair International.

The Learning Suite

The second plan shows how a Learning Suite might look. Figure 1-7 shows a plan prepared for East Side High School in Newark, NJ and illustrates how two Learning Studios can be combined to create a Learning Suite. It illustrates how a Learning Studio-based plan can be quite "rich" as far as activities go. Eastside's Learning Studios are ideal for project-based learning. The two Learning Studios create a Learning Suite that spills over into adjacent areas for both indoor and outdoor learning.

Figure 1-8 is a further development of this concept. In this case, the plan for Tajimi Junior High School in Tajimi-shi,

Gifu, Japan shows a Learning Suite where the boundaries of each classroom are more fluid and easier to change on a day-to-day basis because it is defined by furniture and not by walls.

As the above discussion and plans illustrate, it is possible to create Learning Suites using either moveable walls or mobile furniture. The East Side High School Learning Suite (Figure 1-7) shows Learning Suites that use moveable walls, and the Tajimi example (Figure 1-8) uses mobile furniture. The key difference between these two approaches is that moveable furniture is typically experienced as a friendlier way to create a suite, whereas the moveable wall is more mechanistic and makes the division between Learning Studios more rigid.

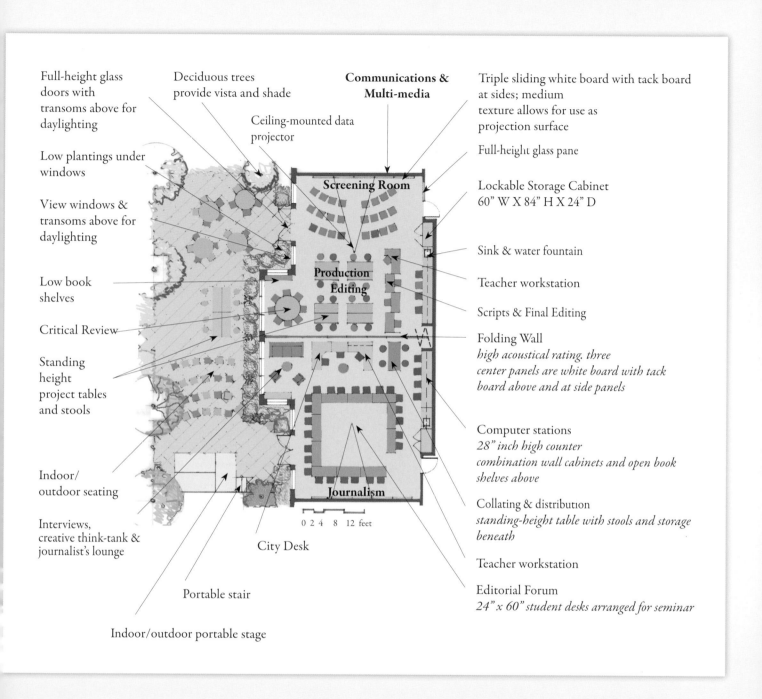

Figure 1-7 labels:

Full-height glass doors with transoms above for daylighting

Deciduous trees provide vista and shade

Communications & Multi-media

Triple sliding white board with tack board at sides; medium texture allows for use as projection surface

Ceiling-mounted data projector

Low plantings under windows

Full-height glass pane

Screening Room

Lockable Storage Cabinet 60" W X 84" H X 24" D

View windows & transoms above for daylighting

Sink & water fountain

Production Editing

Teacher workstation

Low book shelves

Scripts & Final Editing

Critical Review

Folding Wall
high acoustical rating. three center panels are white board with tack board above and at side panels

Standing height project tables and stools

Computer stations
28" inch high counter combination wall cabinets and open book shelves above

Journalism

Collating & distribution
standing-height table with stools and storage beneath

Indoor/ outdoor seating

Teacher workstation

Interviews, creative think-tank & journalist's lounge

City Desk

0 2 4 8 12 feet

Editorial Forum
24" x 60" student desks arranged for seminar

Portable stair

Indoor/outdoor portable stage

Figure 1-7.
Learning Suite design for project based learning for East Side High School in Newark, NJ. Planner: Fielding Nair International. Please note that the placement of several computers along the wall was a school district requirement. This is NOT the recommended way to incorporate technology into a Learning Suite. The preferred method is to use mobile computers that can be deployed anywhere in the room with wireless networking. One or two hard-wired desktops are okay but these should be grouped in a way that encourages collaboration.

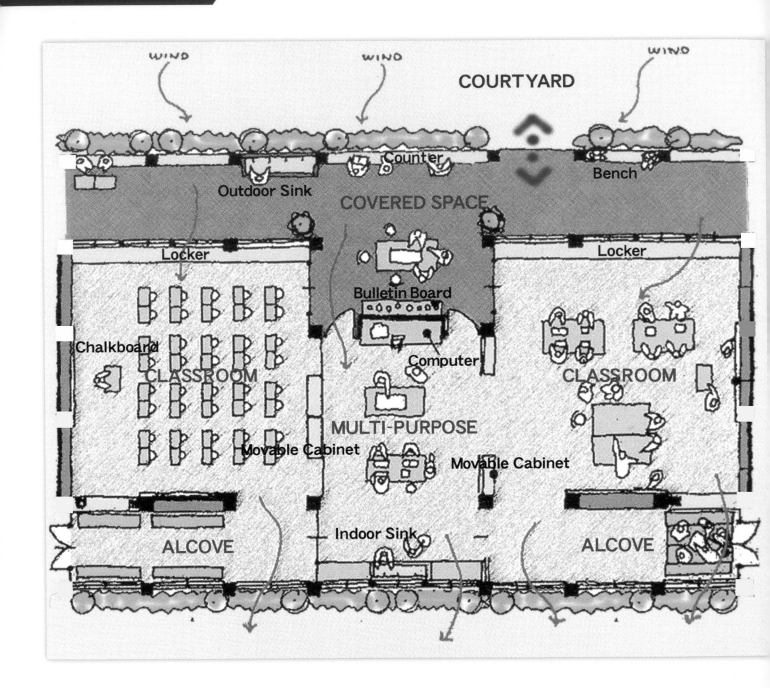

Figure 1-8.
Learning Suite at Tajimi Junior High School in Tajimi-shi, Gifu, Japan. Architect: Atelier Zo.

The choice between the two approaches comes down to philosophical and operational issues. The more flexible furniture-based model is appropriate when the two Learning Studios are more likely to operate as one larger entity with the teachers working in close collaboration with each other. In this type of situation, the acoustical separation afforded by the moveable wall is not much of an issue. Students get used to using their "indoor voices" much as they would in a family-type situation with the realization that the Learning Suite caters to many different learning activities dispersed between the two studios.

More traditional schools that are exploring the idea of team teaching and collaboration between classes, while still wishing to preserve the separation and independence of classrooms or Learning Studios as distinct units, will prefer the model with moveable walls.

Once we have repaired the basic building block of school—the classroom—it is easier to move the school design to a whole new level—still not a completely new paradigm, but much closer than the cells-and-bells model.

Small Learning Community Model

The old standard building block of a school was the classroom unit. A new standard has emerged strongly since the last publication of this book: the *Small Learning Community (SLC)*.

A great deal of flexibility and customization is available within the pattern of the SLC, however it has several features that define it:

1. A 'home base' function for between 80 and 150 students. Capping the number at 150 allows for every person in the SLC to know everyone else. Over 150 and a sense of isolation and anonymity increases exponentially.

2. Those 80-150 students use the SLC for over 60% of their curricular needs.

3. A teaching team assigned to that SLC works in the SLC for over 60% of the time. The number of staff typically associated with a student cohort of 80-150 is a manageable working team size.

4. Physical features of the SLC include: Learning studios set up as learning suites as described earlier in this chapter, small group rooms, a multi-purpose lab (sometimes referred to as a Da Vinci Studio), a commons space that also doubles as a café, cubbies for student belongings, a staff work area, lots of storage, a kitchenette, a resource room, staff and student toilets, a dedicated entry and ample outdoor connections. The idea is that each SLC should be able to cater to most if not all the 20 modalities of learning referenced throughout this book.

5. Students are not restricted in their use of the space, and teachers are happy to let this occur thanks to design that maximizes opportunities for passive supervision.

Small Learning Communities may comprise several or few Learning Studios, however the most transformational practices occur where the Studios are of varying sizes and are used as tools for teaching on an as-needed basis. For example, in the SLC there may be a studio designed for messy work, which is generally accessible by all the students and teachers, but occasionally may be needed by a class or tutorial group for a particular project or demonstration. Similarly, a studio set up for presentation or lecture can be used by anyone whenever they have a need to use that learning modality. The key is that Learning Studios within an SLC are not "owned" by any particular teacher, as is the norm with classrooms in traditional school design. Rather, the idea is for the team of teachers to own the entire SLC and democratically decide who gets to use which space when. That said, each teacher will have a professionally outfitted workspace alongside their colleagues in the teacher's office, which is also part of the SLC.

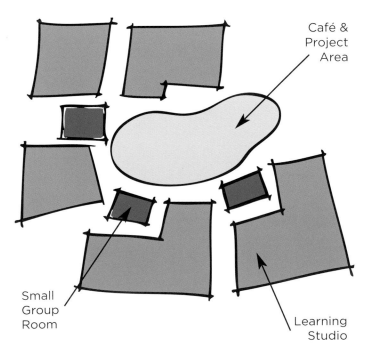

Figure 1-9.
Design Pattern #1e: Learning Studio-based Small Learning Community (SLC).

Learning Studio-based Small Learning Community

Figure 1-9 shows a Learning Studio-based Small Learning Community (SLC). This pattern takes the finger plan and makes it whole so that students occupying an SLC (in a finger arrangement or any other such separate grouping) can truly feel that they belong to that SLC. In the Learning Studio-based model there is still an expectation that most of the teaching and learning will happen in class groups of 20-30.

For example, a Learning Studio-based SLC would contain its own learning studios, its own teacher workroom with the transparency needed for the space to serve as "eyes on the street", its own toilets, its own science lab and its own central multi-purpose social space that can be used for project work, independent study, distance learning, collaborative work, technology-based work and so on. Figure 1-9 shows a simpler arrangement than the SLC described above with Learning Studios clustered around small group rooms and a café that doubles as a project area. But even at this simple level, it is possible to create an effective SLC.

This particular pattern could be modified to show each SLC having its own direct connection to the outdoors. Additionally, each Learning Studio itself could have an outdoor connection. The floor plan (Figure 1-10) and photograph of the Djidi Djidi Aboriginal School in Australia (Figure 1-11) feature another example of how Learning Studios can be combined with other common spaces to create self-contained Small Learning Communities.

We have utilized one more image to represent the Learning Studio-based SLC model. Figure 1-12, the High Tech Middle School in San Diego, California illustrates how a common area shared by an SLC might be used.

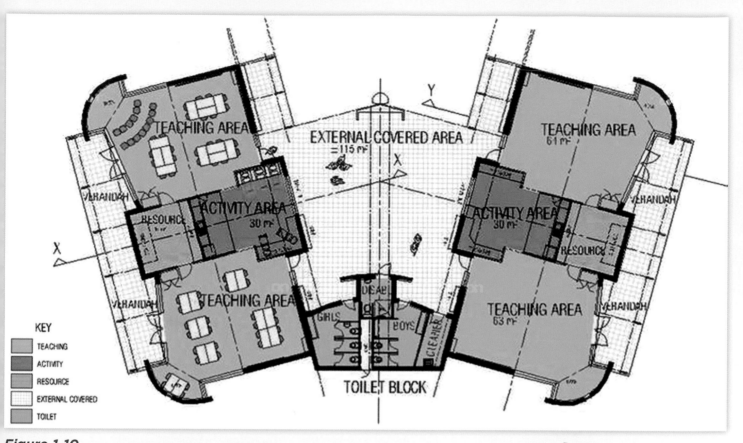

KEY

- TEACHING
- ACTIVITY
- RESOURCE
- EXTERNAL COVERED
- TOILET

Figure 1-10.
Djidi Djidi Aboriginal School design plan based on Design Pattern #1e, Picton, Western Australia.
Architect: Edgar Idle Wade.

Figure 1-11.
Djidi Djidi Aboriginal School, a Learning Studio-based SLC. (Photo Courtesy of Edgar Idle Wade Architects.)

Figure 1-12.
Shared social and learning space outside Learning Studios at High Tech Middle School in San Diego, CA.
Architect: Carrier Johnson. (Photo Courtesy of Bill Robinson Photography.)

SLCs and the Learning Street: In the discussion of Small Learning Communities, the operative word is "small." The idea, always, is to create small groupings where everyone knows everyone else. Of course, the best way to achieve smallness is to make the school itself small—so that the SLC and the school refer to the same thing. However, a majority of school districts that are creating SLCs are doing so by breaking up larger schools into smaller communities on the same campus. It is rare to see truly small public schools that could themselves qualify as SLCs. We are not going to tackle the question of small vs. big in this book—that subject is covered well in the KnowledgeWorks publication "Dollars and Sense—The Cost Effectiveness of Small Schools," which is included in the reference list at the end of this book.

Given today's reality that a majority of America's schools are large and that communities will continue to build large schools, we feel that it is important to see how to preserve the benefits of SLCs in the larger schools.

One way to think about a large school is that it is a small town comprised of distinct neighborhoods—where every neighborhood represents a Small Learning Community. It is impossible to put such a neighborhood/town concept into practice, however, without first thinking about the "connectors" that tie the neighborhoods together. There are many ways in which schools can tackle the issue of connectors—but, whenever possible, opportunities should be explored to make the connectors into one or more unifying elements that give the larger school its identity.

Along these lines, an interesting idea that has been gaining currency is the notion of a Learning Street referred to earlier, which, like the Main Street in most small towns, becomes the unifying element that ties the town's various neighborhoods together and gives the town its identity.

We think that the Learning Street idea is still in its infancy in the school design world, though the idea of unifying elements itself is not new. We have not raised the Learning Street to the level of a specific Design Pattern in this book, but it may well become one in a future edition. For now, we have acknowledged the importance of the Learning Street by including at the end of this book, a slightly modified version of an article we published on DesignShare.com in February 2005.

We have provided a few illustrations of what a Learning Street might look like but we encourage our readers to submit more examples to us that we can share with all of you.

Advisory Model-based Small Learning Community

Moving to the next level of development, we have a pattern that departs entirely from the "classroom" and "Learning Studio" model. Figure 1-13 shows an "Advisory model" of school design.

Interestingly, this model simply represents in the built form what many schools that look traditional have already begun to do organizationally—group students into advisories instead of classes or homerooms.

The Advisory pattern shown here (Figure 1-13) describes how eight groups of 10 to 15 student Advisories might be arranged around a central café and project area. This particular diagram also shows four breakout areas— which could be collaborative spaces with soft seating and an area for presentations.

Each breakout space is shared by two Advisories under the suggested pattern. Since this is intended to be a rudimentary pattern, details have not been shown, such as an Advisory workstation for each teacher/advisor, a closed but partition-able seminar room that can be used for lectures and perhaps for distance learning, separate from project labs and "messy" areas.

The plan for the High School for Recording Arts—Hip Hop High (Figure 1-14) and the photo of students at their workstations (Figure 1-15) shows an Advisory grouping next to a performance area that comes close to representing in built form, what Figure 1-13 is trying to accomplish diagrammatically.

Figure 1-13 begins to take the physical design of school into a functional model where there is a certain hierarchy of spaces, starting with a student workstation at the smallest level and leaving open the possibility of endless configurations of spaces and activities. This model makes learning the centerpiece of the design intent and builds the

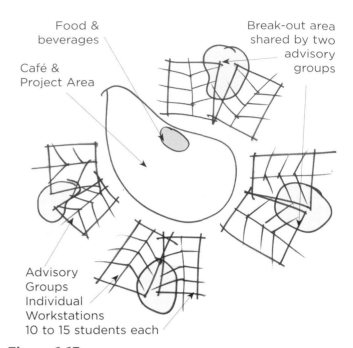

Figure 1-13.

Design Pattern #1f: Advisory-based Small Learning Community (SLC).

plan around learning activities, rather than a theoretically appropriate building block like the classroom. (See the 20 learning modalities discussed earlier.)

The plan for Harbor City International School (Figure 1-16) is another example of the Advisory model and shows how it allows for a much more efficient use of spaces than a traditional classroom model. The Harbor City plan is rare in that it has no corridors and utilizes almost every square foot of space for learning.

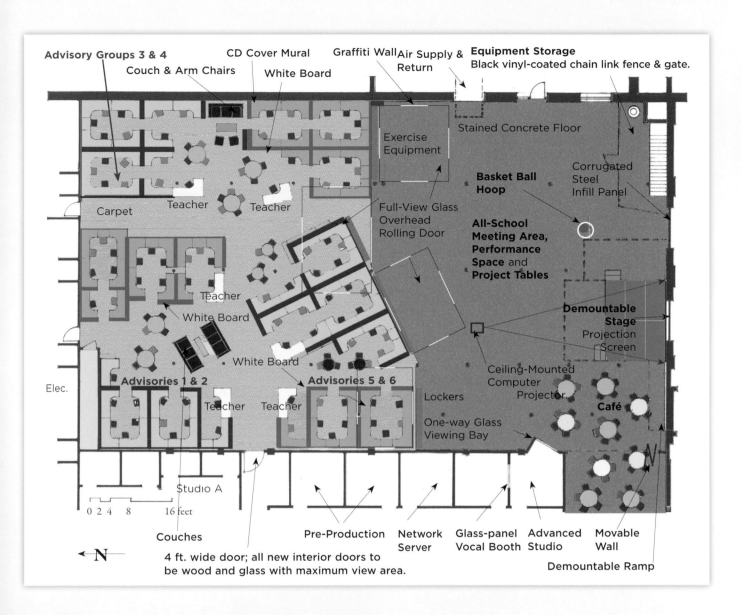

Labels on the figure:

Advisory Groups 3 & 4 • CD Cover Mural • Graffiti Wall • Air Supply & Return • **Equipment Storage** — Black vinyl-coated chain link fence & gate.
Couch & Arm Chairs • White Board
Exercise Equipment • Stained Concrete Floor
Basket Ball Hoop • Corrugated Steel Infill Panel
Carpet • Teacher • Teacher • Full-View Glass Overhead Rolling Door • **All-School Meeting Area, Performance Space** and **Project Tables**
Teacher • **Demountable Stage** Projection Screen
White Board
White Board • Ceiling-Mounted Computer Projector
Elec. • **Advisories 1 & 2** • **Advisories 5 & 6** • Lockers • **Café**
Teacher • Teacher • One-way Glass Viewing Bay
Studio A
0 2 4   8   16 feet
←N
Couches • Pre-Production • Network Server • Glass-panel Vocal Booth • Advanced Studio • Movable Wall • Demountable Ramp
4 ft. wide door; all new interior doors to be wood and glass with maximum view area.

Figure 1-14.
Advisory-based SLC at the High School for Recording Arts (Hip-Hop High) in St. Paul, MN. Architect: Randall Fielding, Fielding Nair International.

Student Workstations
Each learner will have his own workstation and will share a computer with an adjacent learner. Laptop computers and a wireless network will also allow students to work at round tables, couches and on project tables.

Advisory Groups
Each Advisory Group is comprised of 15 students and a teacher. Advisory Groups are paired so that a single teacher may advise two groups.

Desktops
The pre-used desks, donated by a local bank, are 72" X 42". All tops are a neutral color; the colors shown indicate variations in partition colors.

Low-height Partitions
of varying heights, located between desks are constructed of tackable, sound absorbing panels, made from recycled newspaper, and corrugated, wavy metal industrial siding.

Figure 1-15 (left).
Photograph of Advisory groupings showing individual workstations at Hip-Hop High.

Figure 1-16 (bottom).
Advisory-based plan for Harbor City International School, Duluth, MN. Design Architect: Randall Fielding, Fielding Nair International, with Scalzo Architects.

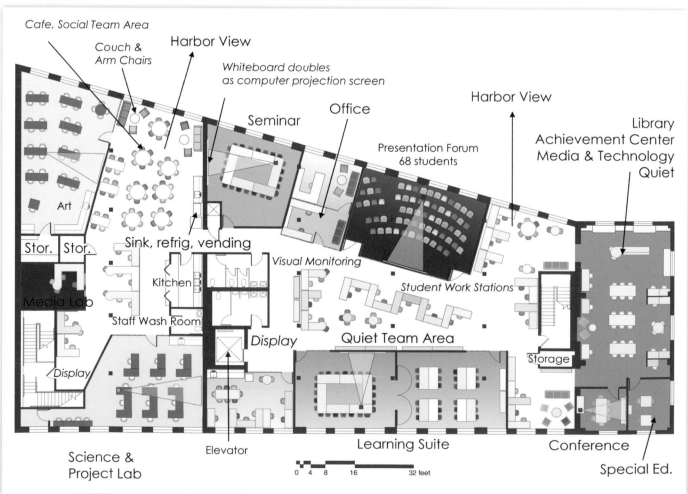

Cafe, Social Team Area
Couch & Arm Chairs
Harbor View
Whiteboard doubles as computer projection screen
Seminar
Office
Harbor View
Presentation Forum 68 students
Library Achievement Center Media & Technology Quiet
Art
Stor. Stor.
Sink, refrig, vending
Visual Monitoring
Student Work Stations
Media Lab
Kitchen
Staff Wash Room
Display
Quiet Team Area
Storage
Display
Science & Project Lab
Elevator
Learning Suite
0 4 8 16 32 feet
Conference
Special Ed.

Community Center Model Small Learning Community

This SLC model is based entirely on the 20 Learning Modalities and functions similarly to the Advisory model, except that students have a variety of different types of settings in which they can set up a temporary personal or group workspace.

The most important thing about these settings is that they are ideal spaces in which to develop self-directed learning skills. After a short period in a well-organized Advisory-based or Community Center Model SLC, students typically change their expectations of the school setting so that after entering the space they immediately get on with their planned work.

Teacher-directed workshops and seminars punctuate the students' days, with the students at upper elementary and beyond able to schedule their own days.

This is in significant contrast to the message of most classroom spaces being the teacher's domain: "Wait until the teacher enters the room and tells you what to do before you do anything. You are not capable of directing your own learning."

A typical Community Center Model SLC comprises one or two Learning Studios, able to be configured for presentation, workshop or small-group work; a wet/messy studio of some sort—able to cater to both arts and sciences in discipline-based and interdisciplinary settings; seminar and small group study rooms; and a large amount of space for passively supervised, student-directed work, ideally furnished with soft seating, larger and smaller table groupings, floor activity spaces and some types of screening devices.

From 1:25 to 4:100 Flexible Small Learning Communities

The traditional classroom model calls for one teacher to manage 25 students in a tightly controlled territory; the teacher is the undisputed ruler, burdened with the task of constant supervision. In contrast, the Small Learning Community model calls for four to five teachers to work collaboratively, sharing a suite of spaces of varying sizes and characteristics with permeable boundaries and strong outdoor connections wherever possible; students have access to additional peers and adults, and teachers have access to each other and environmental resources. See Figure 1-17.

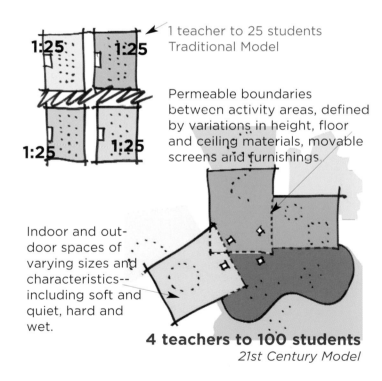

Figure 1-17.
Design Pattern #1g: From 1:25 to 4:100 Flexible Small Learning Communities (SLC). Top—1:25 SLC; bottom—4:100 SLC.

This Pattern is applied in the design of the three new Cayman Islands High Schools. Applying an agile space design that draws its inspiration from the 20 modalities of learning and the ethos of the Cayman Islands, it represents a dramatic departure from the traditional classroom-based high school model.

Even though 1,000 students will be enrolled at the high school, students are distributed in groups of 150 within six home-like SLCs so that each student is personally known by peers and adults and sees the school as an extension of a caring family. Within this context, they are much more likely to grow emotionally and socially and succeed academically. See Figure 1-18.

COMMUNITY CENTRE

The Centre consists of four roughly equivalent open areas divided by a variety of partitioning systems.

Each area has a special function. The Commons is a large group gathering area, is closest to the SLC entrance and has a connection to the outdoor terrace;

The Presentation area is designed for small impromptu talks and lectures as well as formal student presentations. In addition, it has a direct connection to an outdoor amphitheater.

The Collaborative Group Learning area is dedicated to group-oriented project work and acts as a breakout space for the Learning Studio. Reflective Learning area is designed for independent, self-directed learning and also has connection to an outdoor court.

LEARNING SUITE

The Learning Suite consists of two self-contained, acoustically separated rooms that can be joined when desired for team teaching and large group instruction. The Learning Studio provides for large group seminars as well as small group work within a self-contained environment. The Resource Centre acts as an on-site multi-media resource room for students as well as providing a second self-contained learning environment. These two rooms can be joined through the opening up of a movable acoustical wall.

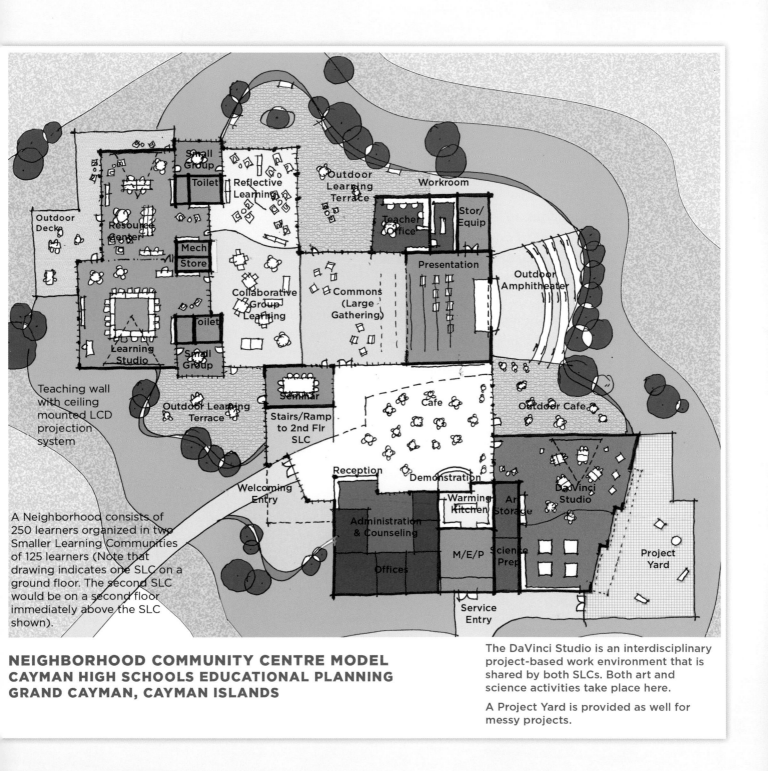

Labels within the figure:

Small Group
Toilet
Reflective Learning
Outdoor Learning Terrace
Workroom
Teacher Office
Stor/ Equip
Outdoor Deck
Resource Center
Presentation
Outdoor Amphitheater
Mech
Store
Collaborative Group Learning
Commons (Large Gathering)
Toilet
Learning Studio
Small Group
Teaching wall with ceiling mounted LCD projection system
Outdoor Learning Terrace
Seminar
Stairs/Ramp to 2nd Flr SLC
Cafe
Outdoor Cafe
Welcoming Entry
Reception
Demonstration
DaVinci Studio
A Neighborhood consists of 250 learners organized in two Smaller Learning Communities of 125 learners (Note that drawing indicates one SLC on a ground floor. The second SLC would be on a second floor immediately above the SLC shown).
Warming Kitchen
Art Storage
Administration & Counseling
M/E/P
Science Prep
Project Yard
Offices
Service Entry

NEIGHBORHOOD COMMUNITY CENTRE MODEL
CAYMAN HIGH SCHOOLS EDUCATIONAL PLANNING
GRAND CAYMAN, CAYMAN ISLANDS

The DaVinci Studio is an interdisciplinary project-based work environment that is shared by both SLCs. Both art and science activities take place here.

A Project Yard is provided as well for messy projects.

Figure 1-18.
Typical Small Learning Community Design for Cayman Islands High Schools by Fielding Nair International.

Renovating Existing Schools to Create 21st Century Small Learning Communities

It is important to stress that high quality, modern learning environments that support all 20 modalities of learning can be created within existing schools. It is also important to point out that renovations to create SLCs within existing schools do not have to be expensive. In fact, they can cost a tiny fraction of new construction and can often be completed in a matter of weeks or months.

One such example is the renovation of Forrest Avenue Elementary School, which was completed by in-house school district construction personnel over one summer for a very modest sum of money. This project had the direct participation of the teachers who would eventually teach in the space. When the Learning Community was created out of a space that previously housed classrooms along a corridor (see Figure 1-19), teachers were able to work as a team instead of singly in their own classrooms.

Interdisciplinary projects and multi-age groupings are now possible and the range of teaching and learning experiences are also increased. The large commons space that was created by getting rid of the corridor is also used for parent and community meetings and after-school activities. See Figure 1-20.

Figure 1-19
Typical double-loaded corridor arrangement prior to the renovation at Forrest Avenue Elementary School in Middletown, RI. Architect: Fielding Nair International. (Photo Courtesy of Jay Litman.)

Figure 1-20.
The same space at Forrest Avenue Elementary School after the summer renovation developed with intense teacher participation and completed largely by in-house personnel. (Photo Courtesy of Jay Litman.)

BEFORE

AFTER

Welcoming Entry

The main entry is a very important element of school design. First and foremost, the entry should be welcoming. It should be inviting and friendly and not institutional-looking or forbidding. We know that community involvement in schools is a key factor in their success and so the community needs to feel that the school belongs to them. This welcoming aspect has to be balanced by the need to secure the entry and separate its publicly accessible spaces from the student areas.

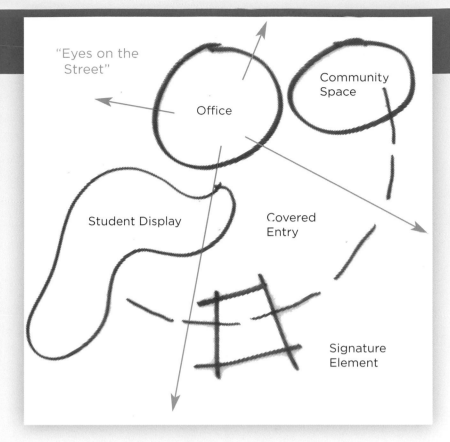

"Eyes on the Street"

Office

Community Space

Student Display

Covered Entry

Signature Element

Figure 2-1.
Design Pattern #2: Welcoming Entry.

Figure 2-2 (bottom left).
A human-scaled Welcoming Entry at Metsolan Ala-Asteen Koulu (Metsola Elementary School), Finland.

Signature Element

A welcoming and inviting school entry will contain some "signature" element that speaks to what makes the school special. For further discussion, please see Figure 2-1, as well as Pattern #23, "Local Signature."

Covered Entry

Whether it has a fabric canopy or a more elaborate cantilevered roof, a covered entry is valuable. Parents often come into school with younger siblings in strollers or have packages under their arms and appreciate a sheltered transition space between the school entry and the street. It is also a place where they might be dropped off or picked up from a car or bus and wait out a heavy rainstorm. Architecturally, a covered entry provides more opportunities for creating a ceremonial quality to the school as a whole (Figure 2-2).

Today, it is common wisdom that all schools need places where the community (and this includes parents) can meet. A space for the community should, preferably, be incorporated as a key entrance element. This serves two purposes. First, it adds to the welcome feeling of the school entry, and second, it enhances the security of the school.

Communities can be welcomed into school in a variety of spaces. Located by the entrance, a so-called "parent/community room" can be a multi-purpose space that allows parents and community members to hang up their coats, have meetings and make telephone calls, make copies, send faxes and access the Internet. Ideally such rooms should also have a mini-kitchenette where parents and community members can make coffee, obtain a soft drink or warm up lunch.

Alternatively, the community room can serve as a workroom for parents and community, and there can be a separate place for informal meetings that connects the school to the outside world. In the case of Cristo Rey Jesuit High School in Minneapolis (Figure 2-3), the bright glassed-in entrance is a place for the community to meet and share ideas each morning.

Office

The school office contains a majority of the administrative functions of the school and is also the main contact between the school and community. For this reason, the school office needs to be close to the main entry so that people who enter the building are naturally led to the place where they can get the help they need. The office space is also associated with centralized student activities such as the guidance suite. This is a space that needs access from the public area for parent conferences as well as from the more secluded student areas. Because of its strategic placement between the public and student areas of the building, the office is ideally equipped to serve as "eye on the street." On the public side, this serves a security function and on the student side, it serves a supervision function where office staff can monitor students engaged in collaborative work or social activities and play. This kind of design enhances safety and security without putting undue or disproportionate emphasis on these aspects of a school's design.

Figure 2-3.
Students greet each other in the Agora (Cristo Rey Jesuit High School, MN). Design Architect: Fielding Nair International.

Student Display

When people enter a school, they need to immediately see that it is a place about students and learning. An entry is, therefore, an excellent place to create and showcase displays of student work (Figure 2-4). By periodically changing these displays, the entry can always remain a dynamic, vibrant place.

Another way in which the entrance to a school can be energized is to have some key student activity area that is visible from the entrance. This area could be a student greenhouse or a project room that shares a soundproof glass partition with the entry. Nothing communicates the purpose of a school better than actual students at work. This concept also relates to Pattern #9, "Transparency and Passive Supervision."

Figure 2-4.
Display of student artwork at welcoming entry, Reece High School, Tasmania.

Home as a Template for School

An educational direction that has emerged in the United States over the past two decades is to make schools look and feel more like homes (Figure 2-5). This pattern is in essence an amplification of Welcoming Entry, and was originally a means of translating research on reducing the stress of new environments in young children. But it also has ramifications for all ages, as traditionally institutional environments are stressful for many people.

The use of terminology such as house plans and neighborhood plans by architects reinforces this trend. Although there is little in the way of empirical research to support the idea of creating home-like school settings, there has been work by environmental psychologists and phenomenologists that suggest the importance of minimizing abrupt transitions between home and institutionalized settings, especially for very young children (Moore & Lackney, 1994). Many architectural elements such as home-like front yards, front porches and friendly entry sequences are all possible ways to reduce anxiety about school and reassure both child and parent. See Figure 2-6.

Creating a home-like atmosphere does not stop at the entrance. To further a sense of comfort, older students can be assigned to a home base with individual desks and lockable storage space. Home bases should be located within a Small Learning Community. Lockers, if provided, should be placed in smaller numbers in nooks or bays in areas where students are likely to socialize in a healthy way. The traditional 9" locker lined up in a hallway is not recommended. Also see Design Pattern #4—Home Base and Individual Storage.

Figure 2-5.
Design Pattern #2a: Home as a Template for School.

Figure 2-6.
Metsolan Ala-Asteen Koulu, a Finnish elementary school, has a multifunctional, residential-scaled entry space. Here, no more than 20 students share a meal in a warm, café-like part of the meandering hall.

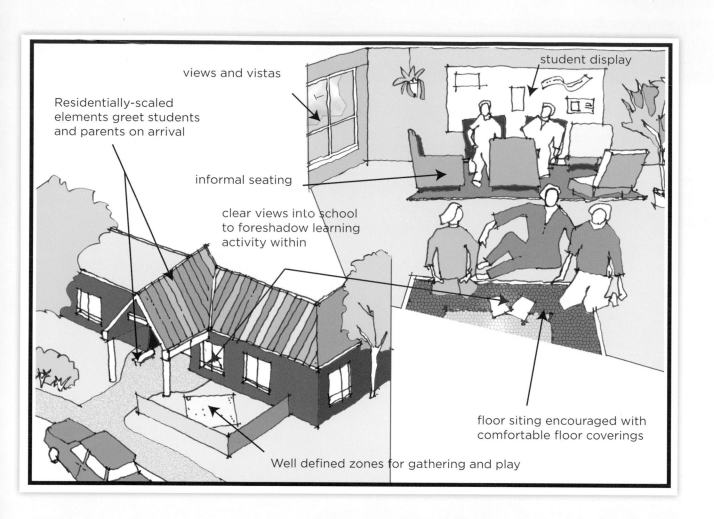

views and vistas

student display

Residentially-scaled elements greet students and parents on arrival

informal seating

clear views into school to foreshadow learning activity within

floor siting encouraged with comfortable floor coverings

Well defined zones for gathering and play

Student Display Space

As discussed in Pattern #2, Student Display Spaces by the entrance can make a powerful statement about the learning mission of the school. Typically, one can never provide enough places in a school for displaying student projects, and every opportunity should be utilized for decorating various places in the school with student work. See Figure 3-1.

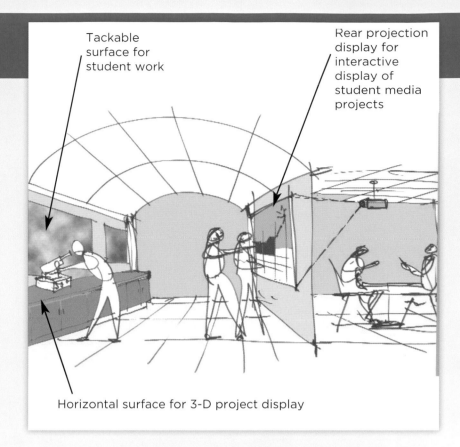

Tackable surface for student work

Rear projection display for interactive display of student media projects

Horizontal surface for 3-D project display

Figure 3-1.
Design Pattern #3: Student Display Space.

Figure 3-2. (bottom left)
Mural in main school entry with student photographs. Bexley Academy, London, U.K.

Not all displays have to showcase student work for it to have a personal connection for students. At the Bexley Academy in London (Figure 3-2), the entrance contains a large display mural with photographs of students and staff who attend the academy.

Another example of an unconventional but ever-changing "display" would be a student-created garden.

Figures 3-3, 3-4 and 3-5 show how Student Displays can become an important and integral part of the learning environment.

Authenticity

The most important feature of a good display is that it is authentic.

This means that if commercial posters are up on the walls, they are either prints of real art/design, preferably with some personal connections for the students in that space, or if they are commercial teaching tools, they relate directly to the students and what they are learning, and they are couched in a display that shows this (for instance,

student work on the topic). Patricia Tarr (2001) described the problems with commercial posters well:

> The flatly colored, outlined stereotyped images of the posters and bulletin board borders talk down to children and assume that they are not capable of responding to the rich, diverse images and artifacts, including images from popular media culture, which the world's cultures have created.

Authenticity also refers to displayed student work and whether or not it reflects personalized and/or authentic projects (also see Figure 2-4). Collections of identical photocopied worksheets stapled to a wall will reflect a program that is not personalized, or that even allows for personalization within a set assignment.

Figure 3-3.
Display of student work at Rulang Pri Primary School, Ministry of Education, Singapore.

Figure 3-4.
Student work displays needn't be collections of near-identical finished work. This display highlights the journey of inquiry at the start of a unit, rather than just a final product (Wooranna Park Primary School, Melbourne, Australia).

Figure 3-5.
Student art lines the walls of the school café at Arabia School, Finland.

Form

Student work displays don't always need to mean paper stuck to the walls, and in many cases this is an inappropriate form of display. Gardens can showcase the authentic work of students and community. Electronic media allow students the opportunity for authentic publication of their work, and can be presented to the community online, in exhibitions and using projectors or large screens in prominent locations. Photographs of students at work show that the process of learning, as much as the end product, is valued by the community.

The best display of student learning is active learning itself. On walking into the school, the community is able to see the core business of the school: students engaged in meaningful activities. For more on this, see the patterns for "Welcoming Entry" and "Transparency and Passive Supervision."

Home Base and Individual Storage

If there is one thing that says "school" louder than anything else, it is the ubiquitous student locker. Despite the nostalgia tied up with them (Can any high school movie be made without the mandatory locker scene?) it is time for lockers to go.

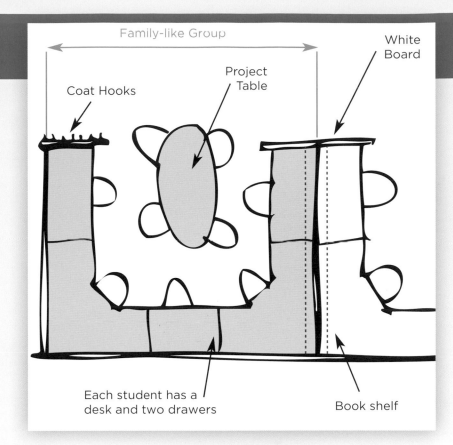

Family-like Group

Coat Hooks

Project Table

White Board

Each student has a desk and two drawers

Book shelf

Figure 4-1.
Design Pattern #4: Home Base and Individual Storage.

Figure 4-2 (bottom left).
Individual student workstations at High Tech High, San Diego. Architect: Carrier Johnson.

So what is the alternative? The most obvious one is the individual student "Home Base" that would include a desk and lockable storage space. See Figure 4-1. Most of the schools that follow the Advisory model have adopted the idea of the Home Base. (Refer to the discussion under Design Pattern #1—Classrooms vs. Learning Studios.)

Student Home Bases at High Tech High in Figure 4-2 provide individual workstations to students. Compare this to Figure 1-14, under Design Pattern #1 which illustrates Advisory grouping with individual workstations at Hip Hop High.

Home Bases can also be provided in spaces that are not as radically different from classrooms as is the case with the Reece High School. See Figure 4-3. Here, the Home Bases are in a typical "Principal Learning Area" or a Learning Studio, according to the definitions set forth in the discussion under Design Pattern #1.

Individual workstations aren't always desirable though, particularly for younger students, and in the case of schools short on floor space individual workstations can remove

some flexibility. However this doesn't mean throwing out the principles of Home Base and Individual Storage.

The main goal when designing individual storage space should be for students to access their belongings under constant passive adult supervision, designing out the tendency for locker areas to become bullying zones, or generally areas in which there is no accountability for time or behavior. See Figures 4-4 and Figure 4-5.

This is easily achieved in a Small Learning Community, where the students occupying the principal learning areas are the same people who keep their belongings there. It can also negate the need for large lockable lockers: Since students are able to provide passive supervision of their belongings, smaller lockables can provide secure storage for valuables on a casual basis, and larger items can be stored in small banks of open cubbies, augmented with coat hooks.

Under this model, the entire Small Learning Community is designed as a Home Base for the students there, with the smaller number of people providing a sense of accountability for each other and each other's belongings.

Figure 4-3.
At Reece Community High School in Tasmania, Australia, students get their own workstation that doubles as their Home Base with lockable storage. Planner and Design Consultant: Prakash Nair, Fielding Nair International; Architect: Glenn Smith Associates.

Figure 4-4.

At Cristo Rey Jesuit High School, the lockers are in small alcoves, augmented with hooks, and are made out of wood, rather than metal. The effect is an environment that respects, and expects respect.

Figure 4-5.
Home Base & Personal Storage. At Scotch Oakburn College, Australia, lockers are wood, rather than metal, and are grouped in small clusters within the Einstein Studios (common areas). These two factors help to eliminate the bullying atmosphere common in traditional locker areas. Master Planner and Design Architect: Fielding Nair International

Locker Sizes, Materials and Configuration

In situations where there is no other way to accommodate student storage needs, make the lockers wider than the 9" standard. Student lockers should ideally be 12"–15" wide and 18" deep. This size permits the storage of laptops, book bags and small student projects in a way that the current 9" standard does not allow.

Use of metal as a construction material for lockers should be avoided. Metal can be easily bent out of shape, and metal lockers are temptingly noisy to open and close. Instead, recycled plastic and/or wood can help to make locker areas less intimidating.

Speaking of locker areas, there's really nothing inherently wrong with having lockers bunched together. However, if the management of the school requires that all students access their belongings at the same time, it makes for an unfortunate crush. Changing this requirement (which could easily go hand-in-hand with a move to more personalized learning) or breaking up big locker sets into smaller groupings are two ways to minimize this issue. Locker/cubby sets on castors also make for more flexible arrangements in small learning communities.

Science Labs, Arts Studios and Life Skills Areas

Life Skills areas represent the "Life" aspect of the four Thornburg

learning modalities: Campfire, Watering Hole, Cave and Life. It

represents a logical coming together of the various other types

of learning. (For more information on the Thornburg modalities,

please see Pattern #15, "Campfire Space").

Figure 5-1.
Design Pattern #5: Science Labs, Art Studios and Life Skills Areas.

Figure 5-2 (bottom left).
Space designed for messy activities, within a Community Center Model Small Learning Community (Wooranna Park Primary School, Melbourne, Australia).

While science and art have strong disciplinary components to them, much of the application of science and art is multidisciplinary. Spaces in which science and art are learned need to have the kind of richness that these disciplines themselves possess.

In schools, typically, science labs and art rooms are the closest thing students have to hands-on learning. In addition, there are the specialized "shops"—though these are only now beginning to recover their rightful place as key learning centers after being relegated for a long time to the "vocational" arena. How would one go about setting up good hands-on places for learning in schools? In this section we will look at design for these kinds of spaces, and we will also introduce the idea of a Da Vinci Studio for schools built according to the Small Learning Community philosophy.

Figure 5-1 shows how a science lab suite may be laid out. The science lab suite contains five components:

1. The Active Lab: This is an area that loosely resembles a typical high school science lab—with one exception. The tables are all moveable, and the services are located along the perimeter.

2. The Student Display: An essential component of the science suite, this is an area where completed projects and projects in progress are displayed as evidence of the real work being accomplished in the lab.

3. Messy Projects: This is the part of the science suite where students get to work on "messy" projects—ones where there may be mud or water or paints involved, for example. This kind of room removes the limits from science projects that may otherwise be placed when there is no messy area to work in. It is a good idea for messy projects space to open into an outdoor work area and for the transition between indoor and outdoor work areas to be strengthened by large doors or a rolling shutter. See Figure 5-2.

4. Soft Seating: This is the "think tank" portion of the suite. It allows a break from the hands-on work done in the other areas. This kind of area for debate and deliberation in an informal setting is often overlooked in the design of science labs.

5. Storage: Storage areas for specialized materials and equipment (not shown in Figure 5-1) are required to be attached to each of the four "zones" of the R&D (Research and Development) lab.

Generic Project Labs

Schools need to contain some generic places for project-based learning where both art and science projects can be conducted. These are large rooms with high ceilings that have power supplied from a ceiling grid. The room would be outfitted with moveable (but lockable in place) work tables that can be combined to create larger work surfaces. See Figure 5-3 and Figure 5-4.

The room itself could be divided into bays and each bay could be dedicated for short or long-term projects. Specialized equipment for woodworking, welding, a kiln for working with clay and a darkroom for photography would be part of or adjacent to the generic lab(s) for both art and science projects.

Technology-Intensive Labs

These are rooms with high-end desktop computers configured for applications such as Computer Aided Design and Drafting (CAD) and Graphic Design. But these rooms should also be set up so that students can gather together for small and large group discussions.

R&D Science Lab Suite

A science lab is not only about doing predictable experiments—it is also about discovery. Students in an R&D science lab do what their industry counterparts do—they work as scientists, doing active research, working collaboratively and testing hypotheses.

Figure 5-3 (right).
Research lab at Grainger Center for Imagination and Inquiry at the Illinois Mathematics and Science Academy, Aurora, Illinois. Architect: OWP&P Architects Inc. (Photo Courtesy of Scott McDonald © Hedrich Blessing.)

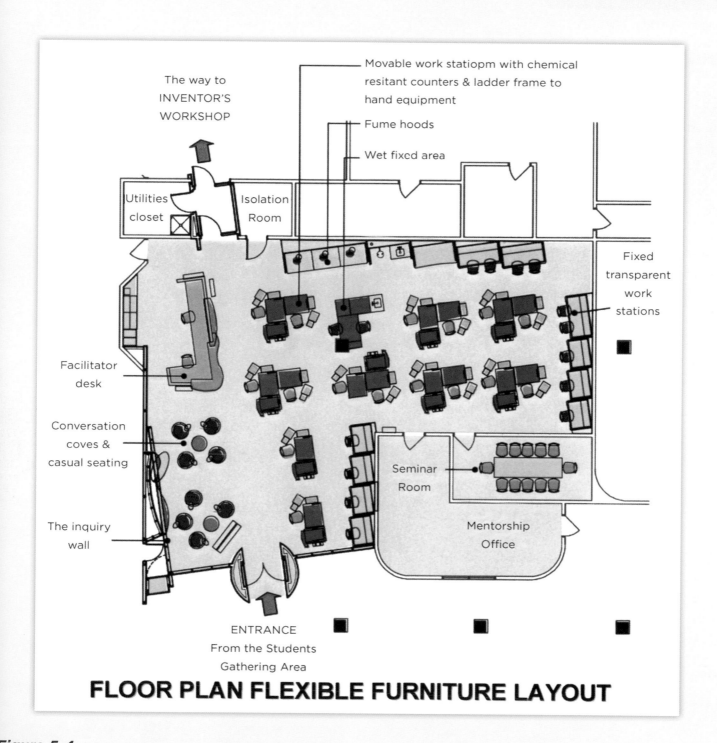

The way to
INVENTOR'S
WORKSHOP

Movable work statiopm with chemical
resitant counters & ladder frame to
hand equipment

Fume hoods

Wet fixcd area

Utilities
closet

Isolation
Room

Fixed
transparent
work
stations

Facilitator
desk

Conversation
coves &
casual seating

The inquiry
wall

Seminar
Room

Mentorship
Office

ENTRANCE
From the Students
Gathering Area

FLOOR PLAN FLEXIBLE FURNITURE LAYOUT

Figure 5-4.
Grainger Center-Floor Plan. Services are located around perimeter to maintain flexibility. (Courtesy of
Scott McDonald © Hedrich Blessing.)

Horticulture Lab—Greenhouse

The greenhouse is a place for active engagement of students in biology, botany, horticulture and environmental science. It is also designed to build environmental consciousness and teach important lessons of sustainability, ecology and an exploration of living science.

An important optional element of the greenhouse can be a "Living Machine." See Figure 5-5. The Living Machine is an ecologically engineered system that combines elements of conventional wastewater technology with the purification processes of natural wetland ecosystems to treat and then recycle the building's water. The system is designed to remove organic wastes, nutrients, and pathogens that can damage human health and ecosystems if discharged. Water cleaned by the Living Machine can be reused in the building's toilets or for irrigation—providing a practical demonstration to students of the benefits of recycling and water conservation.

Figure 5-5.
Greenhouse with Living Machine. Adam Joseph Lewis Center for Environmental Studies, Oberlin College, OH. (Photo Courtesy of Barney Taxel.)

The Da Vinci Studio

Since one of the features of a Small Learning Community is its ability to provide all of its students with the facilities for around 80% of their formal learning, it is important for there to be a space in each SLC where messy work can happen under passive supervision. The Da Vinci Studio is one design solution for this issue. The Da Vinci Studio is able to provide for hands-on learning across all curriculum areas, and support practical work in the formal Visual Arts and Science curriculum areas. See Figures 5-6 and 5-7.

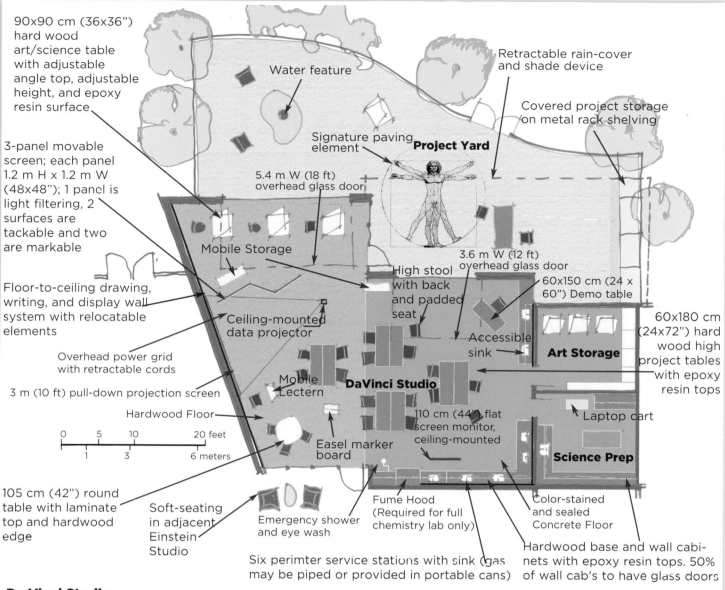

90x90 cm (36x36") hard wood art/science table with adjustable angle top, adjustable height, and epoxy resin surface

Water feature

Retractable rain-cover and shade device

Covered project storage on metal rack shelving

3-panel movable screen; each panel 1.2 m H x 1.2 m W (48x48"); 1 panel is light filtering, 2 surfaces are tackable and two are markable

Signature paving element

Project Yard

5.4 m W (18 ft) overhead glass door

3.6 m W (12 ft) overhead glass door

60x150 cm (24 x 60") Demo table

Mobile Storage

High stool with back and padded seat

Floor-to-ceiling drawing, writing, and display wall system with relocatable elements

Ceiling-mounted data projector

Accessible sink

Art Storage

60x180 cm (24x72") hard wood high project tables with epoxy resin tops

Overhead power grid with retractable cords

3 m (10 ft) pull-down projection screen

Mobile Lectern

DaVinci Studio

110 cm (44") flat screen monitor, ceiling-mounted

Laptop cart

Hardwood Floor

0	5	10	20 feet
1	3		6 meters

Easel marker board

Science Prep

105 cm (42") round table with laminate top and hardwood edge

Soft-seating in adjacent Einstein Studio

Emergency shower and eye wash

Fume Hood (Required for full chemistry lab only)

Color-stained and sealed Concrete Floor

Six perimter service stations with sink (gas may be piped or provided in portable cans)

Hardwood base and wall cabinets with epoxy resin tops. 50% of wall cab's to have glass doors

Da Vinci Studio

Interdisciplinary Studio for 24 Learners and one or two advisors:

In an age where versatility and creativity are keys to success, the DaVinci Studio arms learners with the tools they need to cross departmental boundaries. The studio adapts from a science lab to an art studio in minutes, and also allows multiple learning modalities to occur simultaneously, including:
1. Science Lab and demonstration, including Biology, Chemistry and Physics
2. Fine Arts, including drawing, painting and sculpture
3. Project-based Learning, including individual student projects—building a bridge, a kite, robot, computer or stage set
4. Interdisciplinary—individual and small groupsengaging in independent projects in science, art, and technology simultaneously

Figure 5-6 (left).

At Lake Country School in Minneapolis, Minnesota, science and hands on invention take place in the same studio.

Figure 5-7 (above).

Suggested Design of a Da Vinci Studio. Architect: Fielding Nair International.

Design Pattern 6 — Music and Performance

There was a time when art, music and theater were considered "soft" sciences—less important as it were to getting a good education. The idea was that these things were good insofar as they helped provide a "well-rounded" education but that they lacked the intrinsic value attributed to the academic disciplines like reading, writing, mathematics and science.

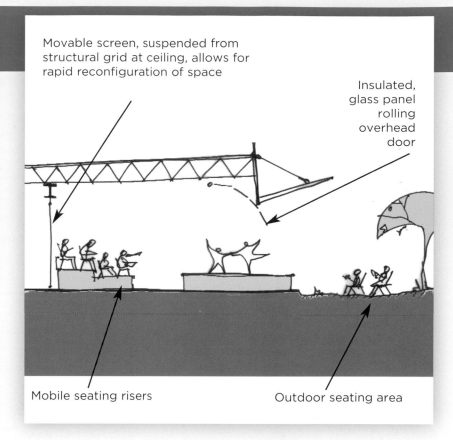

Movable screen, suspended from structural grid at ceiling, allows for rapid reconfiguration of space

Insulated, glass panel rolling overhead door

Mobile seating risers

Outdoor seating area

Figure 6-1.
Design Pattern #6: Music and Performance.

Not surprisingly, school buildings reflect this bias against the arts. Even schools that have the money have relegated the teaching of these disciplines to specialized, often single-purpose, quarters like auditoriums and elaborate music suites.

At the 2005 TED Conference, Sir Ken Robinson made an impassioned plea for creativity to be honored in our educational institutions. He told the famous story of a girl who could not sit still in class, and whose mother took her to see a psychiatrist. Part way through the consultation, the psychiatrist told the girl that he was just going to step out of the office for a few minutes with the girl's mother, and before leaving, he turned on the radio. As soon as they left the room, the girl got up and started dancing. "There's nothing wrong with your daughter, ma'am: She's a dancer. She should go to a dance school." The girl, Gillian Lynne, went on to become a world renowned ballerina, dancer, actor, theater director, television director and choreographer.

How many of our students are written off as non-academics with ADD and prescribed Ritalin to help them comply

with our system of education? How much talent lies undiscovered as a result of this systemic bias?

The old arguments about creativity as being unproductive and of little economic significance are irrelevant today. Daniel Pink, in *A Whole New Mind* (2006) points out that globalization has moved routine, linear tasks to developing countries, expanding the need for more creative, problem-solving skills in developed countries. Much white-collar work today demands creativity in multiple spheres. Ultimately, however, honoring the arts for their own sake as our cultural heritage is most important.

With the growing awareness of how the brain works and the ability to integrate multiple-intelligences theory more fully into the learning experience, it is now evident that the arts are part of, and not separate from, the other disciplines. See Figure 6-1.

We now know for example that art is ingrained in science, that music and math have a strong affiliation and that performance and theater are perhaps the best ways in which literature, history and social studies can be taught.

On top of this, let us also consider that in this technological world, almost everyone needs to become "artistic" with the ability to present ideas using many different media. The commercial value of art and art-related professions has also risen with the new demands for art in almost every field. And so we see art re-emerging as a strong force in tomorrow's school architecture as well.

In order to better reflect and enable the use of creative endeavor throughout the professions and disciplines, schools should enable access to environments for creativity throughout the school, not just in "arts wings." Here are some ways in which we can fully integrate the arts into the planning and design of school buildings:

1. Provide opportunities for students to participate in art-related building features. Sometimes a professional artist will be hired to develop one or more art elements on the building or within the campus. Have students work with the artist to create the artwork.

2. Provide prominent locations for the display of student art projects. (See also Design Pattern #2, "Welcoming Entry.")

3. Provide places throughout the school for impromptu performances.

4. Create a black box theater that can be used and reused for a variety of productions. Connect the theater to a large multi-purpose indoor–outdoor area that can function effectively as a large gathering space.

5. Provide locations where students can build stage sets, paint scenery and develop other artistic props for theater productions.

6. Provide the facility for students to have their own radio station and TV production/broadcast station.

7. Provide the facility for students to produce and publish their own daily or weekly newspaper.

8. Provide the facility for students to work on independent multimedia projects. This can be done by placing high-end computers with appropriate software in key locations, such as adjacent to the library, which students can access and use. Schools that have the funds may also want to attach high-end production capacity to the theater program. These kinds of facilities can often be rented out to local businesses. Community groups and students can also do real-world projects—making the learning experience that much more authentic.

9. Take full advantage of outdoor locations that can be utilized for performance. A "green" outdoor amphitheater can serve as a wonderful performance area as evident from the image of such a space at Swarthmore College in Figure 6-2 but it can also be used as an outdoor classroom, and as an area for group and independent study. A playable musical sculpture is another interesting way in which music and play can be combined (Figure 6-3).

Figure 6-2. (bottom left)
Green amphitheater at Swarthmore College, Swarthmore, PA. (Photo Courtesy of Swarthmore College.)

Figure 6-3. (below)
This outdoor playable sculpture at the Sinarmas World School in Indonesia makes for a nice change of pace by giving kids opportunities to combine physical activity with impromptu musical interludes. Design Architect: Fielding Nair International.

Figure 6-4.
Flexible performance space at High Tech Middle School. (Photo Courtesy of Bill Robinson Photography.)

10. At High Tech Middle School in San Diego, a multipurpose meeting space (Figure 6-4) also functions as an effective theater and general performance space. This is also true at Duke School in North Carolina (Figure 6-5).

11. In the case of schools based around Small Learning Communities, allocate each SLC a performance art facility.

12. Provide discreet areas throughout the school equipped with high quality electronic audio systems, able to be used by staff and students for lessons and projects incorporating music.

Figure 6-5.
Informal performance areas can be easily created in the café-commons spaces at Duke School in Durham, NC. Audience can be seated in rows or cabaret-style. FNI: Master Planner and Design Architects, in association with DTW Architects.

Health and Physical Fitness

Why do so many schools focus so much on sports and so little on physical fitness?

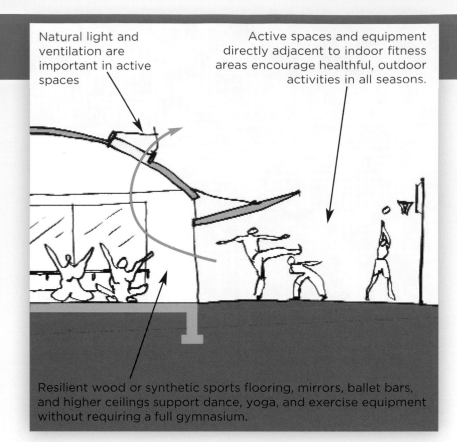

Natural light and ventilation are important in active spaces

Active spaces and equipment directly adjacent to indoor fitness areas encourage healthful, outdoor activities in all seasons.

Resilient wood or synthetic sports flooring, mirrors, ballet bars, and higher ceilings support dance, yoga, and exercise equipment without requiring a full gymnasium.

Figure 7-1.
Design Pattern #7: Health and Physical Fitness.

Figure 7-2 (bottom left).
Physical fitness is important at the Center for Well-Being for the Ross Institute, East Hampton, NY. Architect: Cook + Fox Architects. (Photo ©Peter Aaron/Esto.)

While sports have universal appeal, and schools should encourage all those who are interested to play sports, it is a well-known fact that only a tiny fraction of students who participate in sports during school actually continue to pursue sports as a physical activity after school. Beyond this problem, it is also important to remember that only a small percentage of a school's total population can participate in its sports teams. What happens to the rest of the students? They are relegated to boring "gym" periods with listless (and often forced) physical activity.

In America, it is obvious that public schools are doing a terrible job in the arena of physical fitness. Today's teens are more obese and less healthy than at any time in recent history. For example, in Texas, according to the Texas Department of Health, nearly 40% of all 4th and 8th graders are obese.

The lack of a sustainable physical fitness regimen is not only a health problem, but it also has direct ramifications on the academic performance of students, their rate of absenteeism, and their mental health and overall well-being.

A holistic approach to health and physical education begins with the goal of personalizing healthy opportunities for students, so that their performance is not measured against the elite, but rather against their own personal goals. It means that the focus is on enjoying being healthy.

This is easier said than done. We haven't actually evolved to love exercising. For our ancestors, exercise was an incidental part of everyday life, and when food was scarce, they needed to conserve energy rather than use it up. Now, in developed countries, we are surrounded by systems designed to free us from having to exert ourselves, all the while bombarded by food products that are a poor nutritional shadow of their component parts. Unsurprisingly, this means we've ended up consuming too much food, and exercising too little.

What has this got to do with design? One of the factors contributing to this situation is a well meaning and highly valued collection of designs. Cars, communication devices, cities and their infrastructure of roads, electricity and water, all combine to create a comfortable environment in which we don't actually have to exercise to survive.

Conversely, design can actually encourage, rather than discourage, physical activity. Schools can assist students to develop life-long healthy habits by providing incidental healthy opportunities as well as a range of competitive and non-competitive sports.

A Broader Approach

School facilities (or facilities in the vicinity of the school that are available to the student population) should preferably include places for:

1. Dance and aerobics, yoga (Figure 7-1), kickboxing, Pilates, fencing, juggling, Tai Chi, walking, hiking and bike riding (the last three in areas where outside terrains permit).

2. Indoor activities can include jogging on indoor tracks, recreational swimming and weight training. Gymnasiums can go beyond athletics to create fun, entertaining play spaces. See Figure 7-3.

3. Student gyms need to look more like adult physical fitness centers so that students are more likely to develop healthy, lifelong habits. See Figure 7-2.

4. Supporting active transport (walking, cycling) to school by providing secure, weatherproof bike storage, as well as human-scaled approaches to the site. See Figure 7-5.

5. Places need to be provided in school for a more complete physical fitness regimen. This may include developing the kitchen and cafeteria complex to double as a teaching space for studying subjects such as cholesterol, dental care, drug prevention, blood pressure and body composition, general nutrition, health and cooking. The idea is to teach students that good health involves a balanced diet and a regular regimen of exercise—and that these aspects of living can actually be fun and enjoyable while serving to enrich all aspects of one's life.

6. School facilities should take advantage of the local sporting industries where they exist, and complement

them with facilities of which there is a shortage in the local community, with the goal of providing opportunities for all of these kinds of physical activities.

7. Serving healthy, tasty food in environments that pay respect to the cultural and social aspects of meals. See Figure 7-6.

Community Connections for Physical Fitness

As social creatures, it makes sense that we want to spend our leisure time with others, and for most of us, physical activity is leisure. But school-based sport comes to an end in our late teens when we finish school, and with that, our sporting community disperses as well. For school leavers, there's no obvious route to participation in community sporting clubs.

One solution to this issue may be for schools to operate sporting teams in conjunction with local community-based clubs. This has several benefits. First of all, there is continuity of community for school leavers, setting them up with healthy habits in their adult lives. Secondly, it means that resources are not duplicated across the community: school resources can be used by community clubs, and vice-versa.

Figure 7-3 (top right).
Children enjoy sliding, climbing, jumping and lying down on this big net play feature in the center of Yuyu-no-mori Nursery School in Yokohama City, Japan, which connects the second and third floors.

Figure 7-4 (bottom right).
The Health and Physical Education Centre at Scotch Oakburn College provides students and teachers with several highly agile spaces for organized sports and personal fitness. The wall materials are specially designed to block sound, keeping the rooms surrounding the gym quiet for a range of administrative and learning activities.

Figure 7-5.
Students jog along a tree lined running track at Mypolonga Primary School (Mypolonga, South Australia).

Figure 7-6.
Collingwood College (Melbourne) pioneered the Stephanie Alexander Kitchen Garden project, where children have the opportunity to plant, grow, harvest, cook and eat organic foods.

Casual Eating Areas

One of the big problems with schools is the rigid pattern in which eating is "managed." You will hear the term "three lunch periods" or "four lunch periods" mentioned routinely. The whole food equation in school is simply a logistical one of how to feed *x* number of students within a given period of time within a given space.

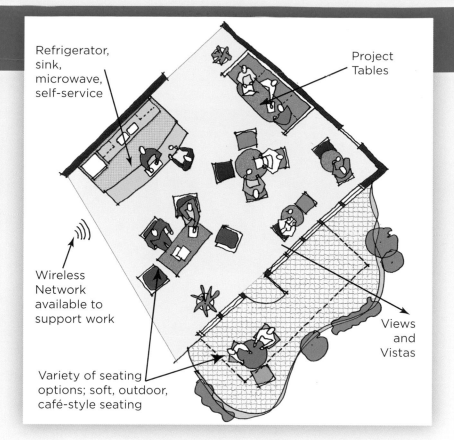

Refrigerator,
sink,
microwave,
self-service

Project
Tables

Wireless
Network
available to
support work

Views
and
Vistas

Variety of seating
options; soft, outdoor,
café-style seating

Figure 8-1.
Design Pattern #8: Casual Eating Areas.

Figure 8-2 (bottom left).
Casual Eating Area at Scotch Oakburn College, Tasmania.

Logistically, it makes sense to have one large hall (or cafeteria as these places are generously referred to) with backless hard seats that can be quickly folded up and kept aside so that the floors may be cleaned up after the students have eaten.

But what seems to make sense logistically does not make sense educationally. The hidden curriculum of such an approach to eating suggests to students that they have no responsibility for or control over their eating, divorces food from the important cultural practices surrounding it, and does nothing to help students discover the processes by which food ends up on their plate—undoubtedly a lost learning opportunity.

Here are some of the elements that would be in place if the whole subject of food were properly handled in school:

1. Students would be able to "eat on demand"—that means, they would have access to food and beverages throughout the school day—with "breakfast" and "lunch" being available during certain prescribed hours.

2. There would be a centralized kitchen, but this would service smaller cafés, which would be more intimate areas than a large cafeteria. See Figure 8-1.

3. Cafés would have round table seating for four to six students each with individual chairs.

4. The cafés would contain some "booths" for more private student meetings. Booths would accommodate two to four students each.

5. Cafés would have picture window access to green vistas whenever possible. See Figure 8-3.

6. Cafés would connect to outdoor eating terraces whenever possible.

7. Each café would be thematically decorated with the themes themselves being temporary in nature and student-selected (also see Figure 3-5).

8. As much as possible, students would be employed as kitchen workers and to service the cafés.

9. Students would help decide the menus and there would be an interesting variety in the food served.

10. Students would take "ownership" of their café by serving food, running the finances of the café and even helping to clean it up every day as in Figure 8-4.

11. The café should be open all day and become a destination of choice for students doing independent study and collaborative work. See Figures 8-2, 8-5, and 8-6. In this sense, it would do double duty as a key learning center in the school as well as a place for eating.

While the above list sounds almost utopian, that is only because it is being compared to what actually happens in school. The list sets forth perfectly reasonable expectations for what school cafés should really be like.

Figure 8-3 (top left).
Café, library and project area at the Avalon School in St. Paul, MN. Architect: Randall Fielding.

Figure 8-4 (above).
"The Cleaning Waltz." Students clean café at Harbor City International School.

Figure 8-5 (top right).
Casual Eating Area at the Harbor City International School.

Figure 8-6 (bottom right).
Providing students with a humane environment for eating encourages respectful and mature behavior. This area, 'The Commons', caters for just one of the Small Learning Communities, and is used during the rest of the day as passively supervised Watering Hole learning space (Cristo Rey Jesuit High School, MN).

Transparency and Passive Supervision

Transparency is a very important concept in school design. Transparent schools convey an idea that learning should be visible and celebrated.

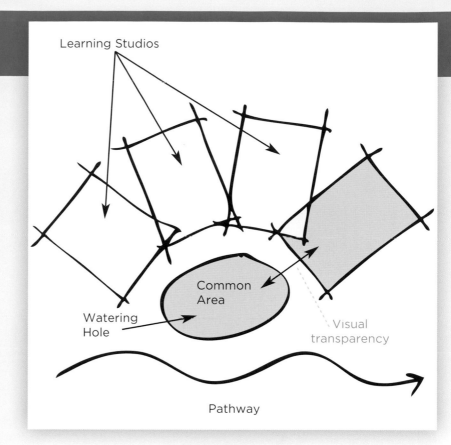

Learning Studios

Common Area

Watering Hole

Visual transparency

Pathway

Figure 9-1.
Design Pattern #9: Transparency.

Figure 9-2 (bottom left).
The power of Transparency. Bexley Academy, U.K.

Basically, Transparency and Passive Supervision is the idea of developing a school with high levels of visibility in both formal and informal learning areas. This creates a sense of openness yet preserves acoustic separation, increases natural daylight in the building, and provides the all-important "eyes on the street" discussed under Pattern #2—"Welcoming Entry."

The Bexley Academy in London, U.K. (Figure 9-2) is a very good example of the power of Transparency at work. It provides a highly stimulating and exciting place for the students to learn and contains numerous areas outside typical classroom settings for both formal and informal learning. The Transparency that has been built-in throughout the school helps create a bright, cheerful place that can also be easily supervised.

Improvement Opportunities

Here are some opportunities to improve Transparency and Passive Supervision:

1. Make the central office and dispersed offices as transparent as possible to improve its welcoming feeling and allow staff to monitor the entrance and supervise areas outside the office where students may be engaged in informal learning activities. When this sort of transparency is put in place, teachers are often afraid that they will be going outside to break up fights. In practice, however, fights are less likely to occur in these places thanks to the atmosphere of mutual trust and safety generated by the openness of the office.

2. Provide visible access from the entrance area to one or more important student work areas like the project lab, art room and science lab. This conveys the learning purpose of the school and showcases it to the public. See Figure 9-1.

3. Provide visibility between classrooms and informal learning areas outside classrooms. This will allow

teachers to monitor these informal learning zones where students may be engaged in collaborative work, learning with technology or independent study. See Figure 9-3.

4. Where corridors are provided, provide glazing into the student work areas to bring light into corridors, reduce the closed-in feeling of the classroom, improve security and create a feeling of openness. Create interesting sight lines from different parts of the school so that there is a sense of drama as people move from place to place in the building. In other words, create a meandering plan as opposed to one that is rigid and predictable. A transparent building allows such a plan to be created with interesting nooks and crannies without sacrificing security.

5. As much as possible, provide transparency between indoors and outdoors. This brings in more daylight, allows students to enjoy available vistas and also encourages teachers to use the outdoors more for teaching and learning due to its direct accessibility and ease of passive supervision. See Figures 9-4 and 9-5.

Transparency is not only about connecting spaces visually but (sometimes) also about connecting them physically. At the Cristo Rey Jesuit High School in Minneapolis, a "garage door" separates a learning studio from the learning commons. This acoustic separation allows the two spaces to function independently. However, for those occasions when the learning community needs to come together as one large group, the commons area can

Figure 9-3 (left).
Transparency between learning spaces at Scotch Oakburn College, Tasmania.

Figure 9-4 (right).
This is a classroom at the Hillel School in Tampa, FL that does not open up to the outdoors.

Figure 9-5 (below).
This classroom at the Hillel School has been opened up to the outdoors through the use of a transparent and moveable glass wall. Not only does this create a day-lighted, more cheerful space inside, but with the glass wall fully opened, the "classroom" now expands to include space beyond its built confines without compromising security. Architect: Fielding Nair International.

be enlarged by opening the garage door and creating one larger space. See Figure 9-6.

As the renovations at Hillel School powerfully illustrate, adding transparency to an older building can immediately make a closed and claustrophobic space feel more open and inviting. In renovation projects, every effort needs to be made to open up walls, taking down unneeded interior partitions that block light and views and bring in more daylight by adding in windows and glass doors. The image of the Scotch Oakburn Library (Figure 9-7) shows how an older space that was renovated by removing internal partitions suddenly feels more open, inviting and better connected to the outside.

Figure 9-6 (left).

This transparent connection between a learning studio and the learning commons at Cristo Rey Jesuit High School in Minneapolis is a roll-up door providing acoustic separation between the two spaces but also the flexibility for them to be fully connected for large group activities.

Figure 9-7 (right).

This renovated library at Scotch Oakburn College is greatly enhanced by how open and inviting it feels—contributed largely by the extent to which it is an open space with strong transparency to the outside.

Interior and Exterior Vistas

Given that so much of learning in school happens in enclosed spaces, there is great benefit to expanding a student's horizons (literally) by creating visible lines of sight that extend as far as possible outside the room. See Figure 10-1.

Figure 10-1.
Design Pattern #10: Interior and Exterior Vistas.

Figure 10-2 (bottom left).
Interior Vistas at Bexley Academy, U.K.

Vistas of 50 feet (15 meters) or more allow us to change our focal length, important to both eye health and comfort.

While the need for exterior vistas is more easily recognized, and school architects do make sincere attempts to create classrooms with good exterior views, the concept of Interior Vistas is less recognized.

With the advent of transparency as an important design principle (see Design Pattern #9), it is now easier to create interior vistas as well. Few schools create interior vistas better than the Bexley Academy in London. Because of the extensive use of glass, there is almost nowhere in the school where students do not have access to generous Interior Vistas. See Figure 10-2.

While the qualitative benefits of vistas cannot be argued, there is a further advantage to creating lines of sight that are at least 50' away from the students' work area. This allows tired eyes that spend hours focusing on things close at hand including notebooks, textbooks and computer screens a needed relief. There is evidence that this kind of relief of looking at objects that are at least 50' away exercises eyes (particularly those of young children) and keeps them healthy. See Figure 10-3.

Any discussion of vistas would not be complete without addressing the question of distraction. The few studies about concentration that have been done would indicate that it is the level of interest in what is happening in class that is a better indicator of distraction than what is happening outside. Also, isn't it easy enough for children to get lost in their own heads when they tune out what is happening in class due to boredom? Fear of distraction is not a legitimate argument for denying children views to the world outside their classroom.

Vistas to nature are particularly important and every opportunity should be taken to orient schools so that the maximum number of students can visually access nature even when they are in their primary learning areas. This was accomplished in the renovated classrooms at the Hillel School (Figure 9-5) and also at Scotch Oakburn College Middle School (Figures 10-3 and 10-4).

There are an increasing number of studies that correlate health and well-being with exposure to nature. In the late 1990s, the Landscape and Human Health Laboratory at the University of Illinois conducted tests on women

Figure 10-3.
The double-height "Einstein Studio" space is the heart of a new student center and looks out at a magnificent view. (Scotch Oakburn College, Tasmania). Master Planner and Design Architect: Fielding Nair International.

Figure 10-4 (right).
Most of the learning areas at the Scotch Oakburn College Middle School enjoy high quality interior and exterior vistas.

residents randomly assigned to different housing projects with different views from their apartments. They were subjected to tests of attention and surveys were done that investigated how the women were handling major life challenges. The results showed that women with views of trees and flowerbeds did significantly better than those with views of concrete. What has long been regarded as a positive attribute of school design—access to views and vistas—has now been scientifically shown to be a very good thing.

Dispersed Technology

In a 2008 survey by the UK group, Campaign for Learning, it was revealed that 52% of the average student's time is spent copying notes from a book or whiteboard. The same survey revealed that what children want more of is to learn in groups, to learn in a hands-on manner, and to learn with computers.

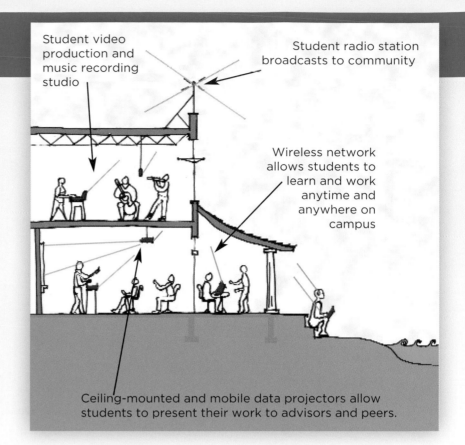

Student video production and music recording studio

Student radio station broadcasts to community

Wireless network allows students to learn and work anytime and anywhere on campus

Ceiling-mounted and mobile data projectors allow students to present their work to advisors and peers.

Figure 11-1.
Design Pattern #11: Dispersed Technology.

Figure 11-2 (bottom left).
Laptop use in an Einstein Studio including powered docking stations: Middle School, Scotch Oakburn College, Australia.

Professor Stephen Heppell, a well known futurist and school planner, estimates that barely one out of every five schools has a 21st century approach to ICT, which involves creating policies that emphasize the possibilities and opportunities for learning that new technologies provide. In these settings, teachers are encouraged to use technology wherever possible for enhancing their classes. The other four out of five are 'locking down', creating policies that treat ICT as a static, rather than a dynamic part of the learning equation.

In this chapter, we will make recommendations for ICT in schools based on current technology. However, any set of extremely strict standards for technology in schools should be evaluated carefully, as most standards become quickly outdated due to the rate of change and growth in this field. The continual challenge is to make sure that ICT helps, rather than hinders, teachers' ability to perform their roles most effectively, and acts as an empowering agent for student learning. See Figure 11-1.

The place for ICT in the curriculum is still under debate in many school communities, where Communications and Technology remain an isolated discipline. There is still often one room designated as a Computer Lab where students go to use or learn these technologies. This model emerged around 20 years ago, and the design was not based on creating effective learning environments, but rather as a result of technical limitations. In today's school and the schools of the future, these limitations no longer exist— ICT can assist in independent learning, anytime, anywhere, and we should no longer be shackled to the Computer Lab model.

Some broad principles to keep in mind for a 21st century approach to ICT:

1. *Students become significant contributors to the continuing evolution of the way we use technology,* not only because it helps them to engage in the learning process but also because their out-of-the-box thinking encourages growth and helps keep ICT usage current. It is not hard to find examples of kids' creative uses of ICT—for starters on sites such as Flickr and YouTube, but also in their use of social networking sites, where users drive the content and page format.

Figure 11-3.
Anytime, anywhere learning with laptops and wireless networking: Pathways World School, India. Planning and Design Consultant: Prakash Nair.

Figure 11-4.
Anytime, anywhere learning with laptops and wireless networking: Reece High School, Australia.

Figure 11-5.
Standing-height, powered-up desktop computers allow students quick and easy access to the Internet and Intranet for small tasks. Note the way support structures are used for this purpose, saving what would otherwise be dead space and a visual hazard. Robert Dean Centre, Scotch Oakburn College, Australia.

Students also need to be involved in the creation of acceptable use policies. Schools that try to pre-guess students and their motivations generally fail at creating effective acceptable use policies because students disagree with them in the first place and therefore do not respect them. Most effective practice is when policy is determined with a partnership of students so that everyone is clear about when and why these tools are being used. The best way of encouraging responsible use of ICT tools in school has been to use them as tools for learning (for example, using texting to communicate on school related issues, rather than banning the use of cell phones or text messages).

2. *Technology infrastructure has to provide trusted storage for the future*, beyond a student's time in that class or school. Students tend to trust the storage at public and widely used networks like Google and Flickr—and if they don't have faith in school storage, they won't use it.

3. *Educators should utilize technology to help extend communication with students outside of the classroom.* There is a range of free software that students already use and that teachers can also use to help communicate with students in instant and direct ways. For instance, MSN or AIM Instant Messenger is used by many students to chat with each other in the evenings. Teachers have successfully used this software in many schools, logging in briefly between 8pm and 10pm to pick up questions from students, or providing "office hours" that are more convenient for everyone involved because students and teachers can "meet"

Figure 11-6.
Peer tutoring, outside, with laptops: Quinns Beach Primary School, Australia (Photo courtesy Keith Lightbody).

Figure 11-7.
Laptop use in a Multi-age Learning Studio: Quinns Beach Primary School, Australia (Photo courtesy Keith Lightbody).

without wasting time in travel. Teachers' online school identities continue the kinds of relationships they have with students in person, online.

4. *A school's facilities must be built to expect and embrace innovation*, rather than simply allow it. Technology is constantly changing and facilities must be built with intentional, directed flexibility and these expectations in mind.

5. *ICT is an excellent avenue through which to engage parents.* Either by watching their children engaged in learning via live video, or by engaging in learning themselves through the power of the school's ICT infrastructure, there are limitless ways that parents can be connected to their child's school, teacher, curriculum and community with the help of technology.

Figure 11-8.
This isn't new technology, but it has been configured to allow users to collaborate with one another. Gaudet Middle School, RI. Architect: Fielding Nair International, Senior Designer: Jay Litman.

Hardware and Logistical Recommendations

A good general rule for allocating ICT resources to schools is to consider the proportion of each student's week that they will spend in various ICT-assisted learning modalities, and to allocate resources to a standard-sized group of students based on that proportion. A standard-sized group of students can be one Personalized Learning Community of approximately 125, or the equivalent number of classes (five classes of approximately 25 students). For example:

- If we estimate that students are likely to on average, spend 20% of their time at school participating in interactive whiteboard-assisted classes, we should make sure that at least 20% of the space allocated to each group of 125 has an interactive whiteboard set up.

- If we anticipate that those 125 students will spend (on average) 5% of their time working with high-end graphics and audio programs, we need to make sure that there are around six high-end personal computers for these tasks.

Of course, this recommendation also requires that teams of teachers work together to share facilities, with the alternative of either equipment sitting idle most of the time, or far worse, some students missing out on access.

Some key principles for the distribution of ICT hardware in schools are:

1. *Hardware should be distributed across the school.* Each unit of 125 students, even in schools where there are no Personalized Learning Communities, needs to have a range of different ICT hardware and software readily and locally available: laptop and desktop computers, peripherals such as printers and interactive whiteboards, and a range of handheld devices. See Figure 11-1 for an illustration of how this distribution might look.

2. *High-capacity wireless and wired networks* should enable a globally connected campus. Internet access is vital in any learning environment, no matter what the predominant subject matter or learning modality is.

3. *A central office for ICT administration, servers and support should be located on each school campus.* Full-time technicians should provide support from these bases; larger schools should have full-time support. Smaller schools should share one technician between two campuses. Whenever possible, involve students in providing technology support.

4. *ICT administrative staff should be provided with daylight-filled workspaces, located conveniently near the central server room.*

5. *Server rooms should be optimally cooled and ventilated to protect the equipment.*

Figure 11-9.
Laptop storage trolleys enable easy access anywhere, anytime, to a pool of shared computers. Reece High School, Australia.

Examples of the types of hardware that can be used in schools:

Standing-height desktop computer stations (Figure 11-5) give students and teachers immediate access to a powered-up computer for quick tasks such as making a query on Wikipedia, checking email or uploading a photo to a class blog.

Seated-height desktop computers (Figure 11-8, note that these are NOT configured to face a wall) provide a similar function to the standing-height computers, with the option of longer sessions and are particularly important for high-bandwidth projects such as video editing. While traditionally located in labs, this is not necessary in an integrated technology model.

Laptop computers owned by students or stored in mobile storage/charging units (Figure 11-9) allow students in a group to use computers for personal learning and projects with added mobility. With laptops, any number of students can use computers at the same time, depending on the kind of project they are engaged in. A one-laptop-per-student scenario is optimal, since it means that students can take responsibility for and have faith in the availability and reliability of their own machine.

It's hard to overestimate how powerful laptops are as learning devices for students today. Unlike office workers, who typically have their own desks with dedicated computers and phones, students are very mobile and their learning activities call for mobility and dynamism. Laptops provide students with tools for creation and collaboration

Figure 11-10.
Laptop use in a Community Center Model Personalized Learning Community, Duke School, NC.

wherever they are: in a classroom, at home, a café, or the local library. See figures 11-2, 11-3, 11-4, 11-6, 11-7 and 11-10 for a range of different spaces that support learning with laptop computers.

Notes on Computer Groupings and Labs

Computer labs are rarely an acceptable arrangement for personal computer distribution. In most cases, if a class of students should all need to use computers for a task, access to a set of class laptops allows for greater flexibility and avoids room changes across campus. If there is no alternative to having a lab, it should be configured with collaborative tables to decrease isolation when using these tools.

Figure 11-11.
In a lab, facing the wall, and deprived of windows—this is how NOT to distribute computers in a school!

Where desktop computers are provided, either in labs or in small groups in non-labs, care must be taken to ensure that they are arranged in a manner conducive to learning. Any space occupied by people for extended periods of time must have windows with a view and significant daylight as this is essential for health and productivity. While it may be tempting to design labs without windows for fear of glare, it is far healthier to incorporate windows and use translucent shading devices to cut glare when required. In addition, no computer user should be seated facing a wall. While convenient from a technical standpoint, this does nothing to encourage collaboration and is reminiscent of the days of children facing the wall as punishment. See Figure 11-11 for exactly how **not** to set up a computer lab! Contrast this to Figure 11-8 where the users are facing each other, rather than a wall.

Handheld Devices

Cameras, mobile phones, GPS units and MP3 players, and the devices that offer several of these functions, offer a huge number of possibilities for use in education.

Handheld devices enable participants to create multisensory content for community or global collaborations via the Internet. Students also gain opportunities for higher-order thinking when they go behind the scenes of digital media and learn to express ideas by producing their own digital pictures and video.

Handheld devices can also be used for flexible content delivery. This might mean teacher or lecturer-created audio or other free academic podcasts. With greater bandwidth, a quality store of validated digital educational resources can provide teachers and students with significant additional learning resources, which is helpful for teachers interested in providing students with more customized learning options. Some schools are also using short digital video clips to document student progress and show the goals that students have met.

High Capacity Video Cameras (Figures 11-12 and 11-13) allow students to record video and create their own movies. Videos can be used as a supplement to projects, reports or presentations, or students can use cameras to help in art classes or to create their own films. Videos can be shared online for distance collaboration or as a way to engage families and communities.

Digital Still Cameras with Video Capability— Photography can be used in much the same way as Video with the added benefits of print.

MP3 Players: Taking advantage of the huge storage capacity of the iPod means that students are able to carry all the learning content they need around in their pockets, instead of trying to carry around many heavy textbooks, causing strain and back problems for many students. Podcasts or videos by their own teachers, other students, and outside experts allow students to learn anytime, anywhere, at their own pace. Students can choose the texts that are of specific interest to them and are able to carry them around easily and access them at their convenience. Podcasts and video also allow students to play and view their own and others' projects anytime, anywhere.

MP3 players also provide a range of different learning opportunities for beginning/emerging readers and speakers of different languages.

Figure 11-12.
Learning with high-capacity video cameras at Reece High School, Australia.

Positive outcomes from the 2006 iPod trial at Heathmont College in Australia show:

- improved student engagement, attention span and behavior

- 20%-30% increase in grades

- increased access to higher-order thinking

- less reliance on textbooks

- pupils better able to work at their own pace and take more control over their learning

Some examples of schools that have successfully incorporated iPods as a learning tool include Western Academy in Beijing; Empire High School in Arizona; Heathmont College in Melbourne, Australia; and Gracemount High School in Edinburgh, UK.

Figure 11-13.
Learning with high-capacity video cameras at Robert Dean Centre, Scotch Oakburn College, Australia.

Distance Learning Facilities

Distance learning facilities are rooms set up specifically for the purpose of remote two-way communication. This technology can be used to include remote guest lecturers and speakers to help teach classes, as well as to help link groups of students to each other for collaborative learning when not in the same physical space. Students who could benefit most from the facility are those in more remote and often smaller schools, where the range of local experts is significantly smaller than in larger schools and campuses.

The design of a studio intended to properly support two-way live interactive instruction through videoconferencing can be quite complex. The layout and design issues will vary widely depending on room size and dimensions, as well as its intended use or uses. It is important that components can be easily upgraded. Some components will be suitable for many years, such as high-quality speakers and microphones. Other components will reach obsolescence far earlier.

At the low end of the cost scale, a simple room equipped with a large monitor with a central shared camera and microphone meets basic needs. At the higher end, and particularly if a facility is to be rented out after school hours or used for adult education, it should be designed so that every student has access to a microphone. In such facilities, wall-mounted cameras would track and focus on

Figure 11-14.

Students using an interactive whiteboard: Middle School, Scotch Oakburn College, Australia.

individual speakers or students as well as the room at large making the distance learning experience as close to face-to-face, on-site learning as possible.

Interactive Whiteboards (IWBs) and Data Projectors

Interactive whiteboards (Figure 11-14) can be a great addition to a learning space wherever there is a plan and willingness for them to be used to their full advantage by a teacher or group of teachers.

In any setting interactive whiteboards are deployed, comprehensive professional development in their use is necessary, including talks by accomplished IWB users and action research teams within the school. The investment will be worth nothing if teachers are not given the support and encouragement they need to explore options for using the boards, and regular data projectors may as well be installed instead.

Permanent audio facilities need to accompany any IWB, data projector or large monitor.

Display Monitors

Each SLC/Cluster should have a 50-inch flat-screen display monitor for DVD viewing and student presentation.

Printers, Scanners & Copiers

The location of printers, scanners or copiers, especially when these are shared resources, needs to be easily accessible so that students will not interrupt any direct instruction. In a SLC this is likely to be a café or commons area. In a cluster of five classrooms/learning studios this could be a modified corridor or a commons area.

Intranets/ Media Storage, Retrieval and Distribution

In most school settings, particularly where students do not have their own computers, it is very important that a school Intranet allows secure, easy access for each student to his/her own personal portfolio of current and completed work, and any centrally located electronic media.

Administrative school matters can also be communicated to parents and students online via email or other external connections.

Personal electronic portfolios of work, stored on the school's intranet can be shared with parents, teachers and where appropriate, peers, and can be enabled to allow feedback which can help students to improve the quality of their work, and help advisors/teachers track students' progress.

Students' electronic portfolios may also be shared with prospective employers or colleges at each student's discretion.

As is the case with any aspect of school design, the ultimate goal in providing ICT facilities is to provide as many opportunities as possible for learning in as many different modes as possible. Schools that provide students with the right tools—tools that meet the students in their worlds—and create a culture of collaboration and creativity are continually delighted by the new methods students devise for their own learning.

Indoor-Outdoor Connection

Human beings are genetically engineered to be outdoor animals and the need to be connected to the outdoors is never stronger than when we are young.

Kitchen Garden

Fish hatchery

Composting

Paths and site development can be oriented to animal habits, encouraging existing species to remain and additional ones to return.

Figure 12-1.
Design Pattern #12: Indoor-Outdoor Connection. A nature trail, while supporting studies in biology, ecology, botany and animal behavior, can also serve as a running track, becoming a vital part of a physical education program.

Figure 12-2 (bottom left).
Qatar Foundation Elementary School-early childhood playground. Qatar.

Figure 12-1 shows how a nature trail, running track and kitchen garden can be integrated so that the outdoors becomes a natural extension of indoor learning. Every opportunity should be explored to create strong connections between indoor spaces and outdoor areas such as learning terraces, kitchen gardens, shaded reading areas, natural creeks and other water features, nature trails, and playfields.

In most parts of the world, students are expected to spend their break times outdoors. Chances are there's no problem with this, but we need to make sure that we reciprocate with high quality outdoor environments—high quality enough even for teachers to choose to bring students outside during class times!

Outdoor learning can take many forms. The paired Learning Studios developed for East Side High School in Newark (see Figure 1-7 in Design Pattern #1) works well because of the seamless connection it makes between indoor and outdoor learning spaces. The same is true of the concept personal learning community plan for Meadowdale Middle School (Figure 12-3).

We had discussed earlier how the Hillel School in Tampa can now use the outdoors as an extension of classroom activities after installing a transparent glass wall seamlessly connecting indoor and outdoor spaces. See Figure 9-5.

At the simplest level, it takes the classroom learning itself to an outdoor setting where the teacher and students can participate in many of the activities that they might have done indoors such as participate in seminars.

But outdoor settings allow other kinds of learning to happen that could not take place indoors. It is an excellent arena for large projects and messy activities, for gardening, for nature walks, to care for animals, and, with younger children, to play on specialized equipment that develops large motor skills as in Figure 12-2.

Interior Courtyards represent an effective method to extend indoor learning. However, courtyards that are open on one side like the one at Tajimi Junior High School (Figure 12-4) are better places to be in because they feel cozy and inviting and not prison-like.

Figure 12-3.

Strong Indoor-outdoor Connections are illustrated in this concept diagram by Fielding Nair International for a Personal Learning Community at Meadowdale Middle School in Lynnwood, WA.

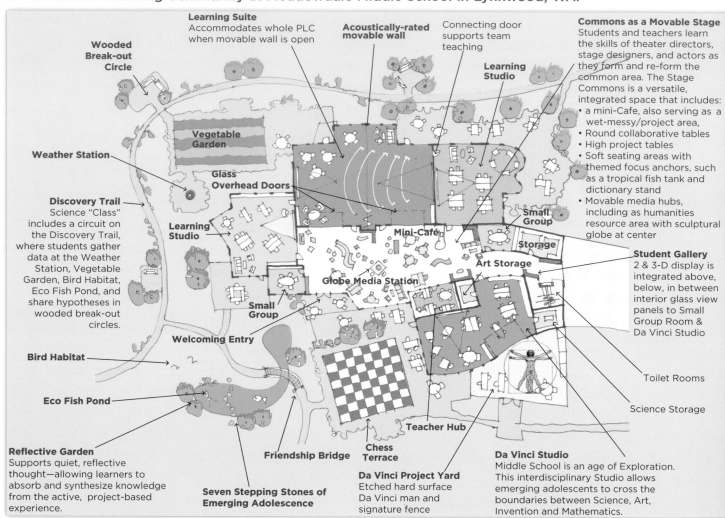

Learning Suite
Accommodates whole PLC when movable wall is open

Acoustically-rated movable wall

Connecting door supports team teaching

Learning Studio

Commons as a Movable Stage
Students and teachers learn the skills of theater directors, stage designers, and actors as they form and re-form the common area. The Stage Commons is a versatile, integrated space that includes:
• a mini-Cafe, also serving as a wet-messy/project area,
• Round collaborative tables
• High project tables
• Soft seating areas with themed focus anchors, such as a tropical fish tank and dictionary stand
• Movable media hubs, including as humanities resource area with sculptural globe at center

Wooded Break-out Circle

Vegetable Garden

Weather Station

Glass Overhead Doors

Discovery Trail
Science "Class" includes a circuit on the Discovery Trail, where students gather data at the Weather Station, Vegetable Garden, Bird Habitat, Eco Fish Pond, and share hypotheses in wooded break-out circles.

Learning Studio

Mini-Café

Small Group

Storage

Art Storage

Student Gallery
2 & 3-D display is integrated above, below, in between interior glass view panels to Small Group Room & Da Vinci Studio

Small Group

Globe Media Station

Welcoming Entry

Bird Habitat

Toilet Rooms

Science Storage

Eco Fish Pond

Teacher Hub

Reflective Garden
Supports quiet, reflective thought—allowing learners to absorb and synthesize knowledge from the active, project-based experience.

Friendship Bridge

Chess Terrace

Seven Stepping Stones of Emerging Adolescence

Da Vinci Project Yard
Etched hard surface Da Vinci man and signature fence

Da Vinci Studio
Middle School is an age of Exploration. This interdisciplinary Studio allows emerging adolescents to cross the boundaries between Science, Art, Invention and Mathematics.

Figure 12-3a. Playful Edges (left)
A wrought iron fence defining the Da Vinci Project Yard may be constructed by a school community-arts partnership. Students can participate in the identification of local signature themes while learning about design, welding and fabrication in a project-based curriculum.

Figure 12-3b. Commons as a Movable Stage (top right)

Figure 12-3c. Chess as Outdoor Theater (bottom right)
Integrating math, social learning, and active, outdoor activities. (Kneeler Design, Victoria, Australia; Photo Courtesy: Silvi Glattauer).

While the Tajimi example works well for middle and high school students, elementary school students also need direct connections from primary learning areas to the outside but such connections need to be more secure and directly supervisable. Good examples are the outdoor learning areas directly adjacent to classrooms at the Qatar Foundation School (Figure 12-5) and the fenced-in outdoor play area at Eltham College (Figure 12-6).

A dilemma that school designers often face has to do with upper story learning areas. By and large, such areas are built without providing any direct outdoor access. However, upper stories should also be planned in a way that they can have outdoor access onto terraces and generously sized balconies. Medlock School shows one simple and low-cost way in which to provide outdoor space on an upper floor (Figure 12-7).

At the PK Yonge Developmental Research School in Gainesville, Florida, a new elementary school will feature extensive connections between learning communities and outdoor learning areas as well as strong connections to an environmentally-rich creek that runs across the school campus (Figure 12-8).

Another idea for outdoor space that schools almost never utilize is the provision of landscaped horticulture gardens where students can relax and unwind. Sinarmas World Academy in Indonesia does a great job in this regard (Figure 12-9).

Figure 12-4 (above).
Open interior courtyard, which serves as circulation, social and independent study space at Tajimi Junior High School. Tajimi-shi, Gifu, Japan.

Figure 12-5 (top right).
Strong Indoor-Outdoor Connection at Qatar Foundation Elementary School.

Figure 12-6 (bottom right).
Outdoor Learning space at Eltham College, Melbourne, Australia.

Figure 12-7 (above).
Multi-story buildings are no excuse for not having outdoor learning spaces. The second floor of Medlock School, Manchester, UK, offers an inviting, colorful Learning Terrace.

Figure 12-8 (top right).
PK Yonge Developmental Research School, Gainesville, FL. Rendering shows view from the south side of the elementary school building with views of the deck patio, the outdoor café and the creek discovery platform. Architect: Fielding Nair International.

Figure 12-9 (bottom right).
View of landscaped gardens at Sinarmas World Academy that provide a soothing retreat to students from the rigors of academic life.

Furniture: Soft Seating

On those rare occasions where students are given an opportunity to comment on the quality of their learning environment, one answer always seems to make the cut—"give us more Soft Seating."

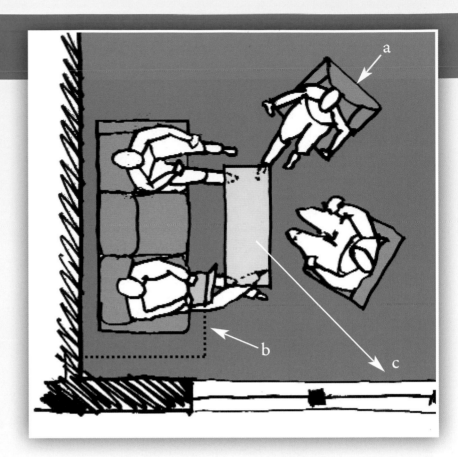

Figure 13-1.

Design Pattern #13: Furniture: Soft Seating. a) Movable seating allows learners to modify their environment; b) Electrical power, wired and wireless connections turn soft seating areas into high powered work spaces; c) Vistas to the city, community activities or nature foster broad-based rather than narrowly referenced thinking.

Figure 13-2 (bottom left).
Students lounge in the Commons at Scotch Oakburn College in Tasmania.

Almost every surface in school that students sit on is hard. To make things worse, the hard surfaces are rarely designed to be ergonomic and almost never are they designed for students to sit in them for hours and hours each day as is the case. Some estimate that as many as 50% of all Americans have back problems. It would be interesting to find out how much of this can be attributed to the unhealthy seating arrangements during 12 years of school.

It is not unusual for a school board that spends $30 million on a school building to spend $30 on a student chair within that brand-new building. This is like paying $10,000 for a stereo system and then listening to it on $10 speakers.

In the same way that adults need soft, ergonomic seating to make it possible for them to be productive at work, so also our students need soft, ergonomic seating to enhance their ability to be good learners.

Reconsider the need for every student in the school to be simultaneously seated on identical chairs. With a variety of furniture available, students are able to spend parts of each day standing, sitting on the floor and sitting on lounge chairs in addition to time on regular chairs, of which there are now many ergonomic options available.

Preferably, all seats in primary learning areas should be upholstered. Alternatively, there needs to be at last a few soft seats in the room—perhaps an armchair or two and a small couch as in Figure 13-1. In addition, Soft Seating needs to be available in other areas of the school building where students study independently or congregate in small groups. See Figures 13-2 through 13-5.

Figure 13-3 (top left).
Soft Seating in the music suite at Lake Country School, Minneapolis, MN.

Figure 13-4 (bottom left).
Soft Seating at Harbor City International School.

Figure 13-5 (above).
Throw pillows create a comfortable and playful soft seating corner in the library at Sinarmas World Academy in Indonesia.

Flexibility, Adaptability and Variety

Earlier in this book, we identified 20 different kinds of learning modalities that school buildings need to support. With flexible spaces to accommodate as many of these modalities of learning into any given space as possible, we can move away from a model of single-purpose spaces to multifunctional areas.

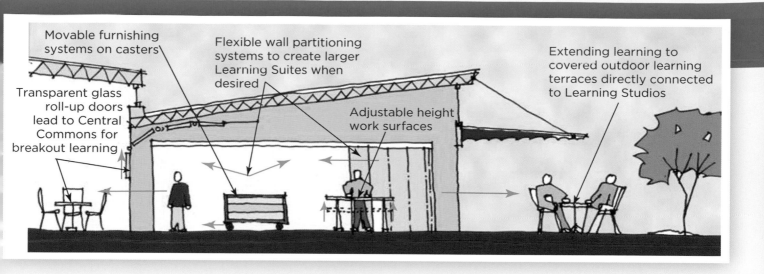

Movable furnishing systems on casters

Transparent glass roll-up doors lead to Central Commons for breakout learning

Flexible wall partitioning systems to create larger Learning Suites when desired

Adjustable height work surfaces

Extending learning to covered outdoor learning terraces directly connected to Learning Studios

Figure 14-1.
Design Pattern #14: Flexibility, Adaptability and Variety.

Figure 14-2 (bottom left).
This café at the Sinarmas World School in Indonesia is a very flexible space. It can serve as a cave space, as a watering hole space, for small and large group meetings, for informal presentations, for independent study and learning with technology.

"Flexible spaces" used to be understood as simply moveable walls between classrooms. The moveable walls provided little or no flexibility in a day-to-day sense: they would generally be either open or closed for a whole year or more. Flexibility is more sophisticated than this. It helps to think about modification of spaces using the ideas of *Adaptability, Flexibility* and *Variety*. See Figure 14-1.

Adaptability is as much about what *can't* be changed as what can be changed. By designing to accommodate human need, rather than current practice, we honor the humanity of students. What stays constant is the building ergonomics: natural ventilation, natural light, acoustics and indoor-outdoor connections. Other aspects of the building, such as the size of the rooms, should be able to be changed if necessary, over the years.

Creating multifunctional spaces is easier said than done. For example, one of the most common multifunctional spaces in school is the "cafetorium," which is a cafeteria with a stage at one end. While this kind of space may work sometimes, user communities are often unhappy with this particular combination of uses. With the number of hours

that are scheduled for food service, the utility of the space as a place for performances, music and drama is severely compromised. On top of that, it is hard to reconcile the different ambiances that cafeterias and performance spaces need. Flexibility needs to start with the primary learning areas or classrooms where so much of a student's time is spent.

One of the learning modalities that is most difficult to accommodate in a traditional school is team-teaching, and the open classrooms movement of the '70s attempted to rectify this situation through use of moveable walls. The problem with this kind of flexibility was that it tended only to be used from year to year according to teacher preference, rather than daily according to learning needs. The lesson from this is to ensure that space is readily available for working with a number of different sized groups of students and teachers in different modalities, with a common feature of passive supervision, rather than teacher control.

In Design Pattern #1 are examples of highly flexible Learning Studios that can accommodate a variety of

Adaptability	Flexibility	Variety
Core structures designed according to ergonomic principles rather then current practices (e.g. Small Learning Communities, use of daylight, natural ventilation)	Allows building users to change the space themselves	Allows users to change the quality of their space simply by moving—for instance, from a Campfire space to a Cave space to a Watering Hole space to an active learning space to an outdoor amphitheater
Non load-bearing interior walls that can easily be removed	Moveable walls and acoustic partitions, swing walls, overhead garage doors, furniture on castors all enable this	Central to the idea of the Community Center Model SLC.
Allows for change over a period of years or decades	*Allows for change over the course of each day or for many weeks depending on the kinds of learning activities under way*	*Allows for instant change and for learning activities to be perfectly matched to environments that best suit them*

Table 14-1.

Distinctions between adaptability, flexibility, and variety in terms of space, structure and change.

learning modalities. Refer to Figure 1-6, the plan for the Advanced Learning Environment module, and to Figure 1-7, the East Side High School plan.

The plan on the Reece High School campus of Building 7 (Figure 14-3) can be reconfigured in many different ways. This building can house 500 guests and a distance-learning program, but can also be used for dance and music and catering and sewing and various other programs on a daily basis. The building also has strong outdoor connections. Re-configuration appears to be an onerous task but is actually used as a learning opportunity: a small group of students act as hall custodians and are trained (by older group members) in the technical operation of the building.

The award-winning Shitara Middle School in Japan also paid a lot of attention to the idea of flexibility as evident from the design in Figure 14-4.

People may not associate a lobby or commons space with an ideal space for artistic ventures, but at Sinarmas World Academy, students happily brush up on their skills in a flexible commons space. See Figure 14-5.

By creating an ambiance that varies greatly from a typical school cafeteria, Sinarmas World School in Indonesia has created a flexible café space that can be used for a variety of activities. See Figure 14-2.

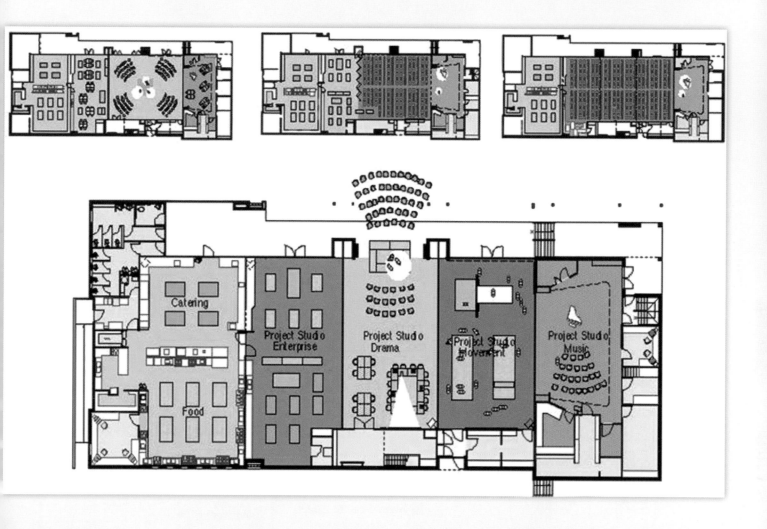

Figure 14-3.
Flexible all-purpose Building #7 at Reece Community High School in Tasmania, Australia.

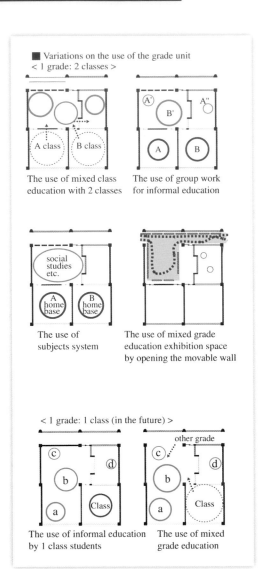

■ Variations on the use of the grade unit
< 1 grade: 2 classes >

The use of mixed class education with 2 classes

The use of group work for informal education

The use of subjects system

The use of mixed grade education exhibition space by opening the movable wall

< 1 grade: 1 class (in the future) >

The use of informal education by 1 class students

The use of mixed grade education

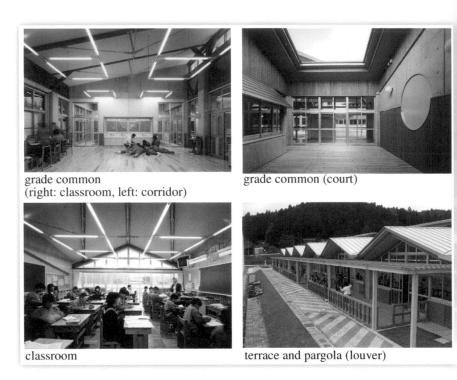

grade common
(right: classroom, left: corridor)

grade common (court)

classroom

terrace and pargola (louver)

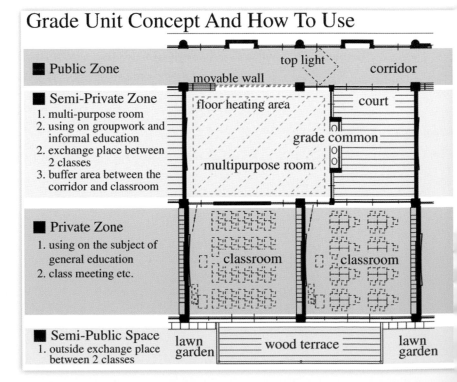

Grade Unit Concept And How To Use

■ Public Zone

■ Semi-Private Zone
1. multi-purpose room
2. using on groupwork and informal education
2. exchange place between 2 classes
3. buffer area between the corridor and classroom

■ Private Zone
1. using on the subject of general education
2. class meeting etc.

■ Semi-Public Space
1. outside exchange place between 2 classes

top light
movable wall
corridor

floor heating area
court

multipurpose room
grade common

classroom
classroom

lawn garden
wood terrace
lawn garden

Figure 14-4 a, b & c.

Flexible groupings for grade unit. Shitara Middle School, Shitara Town, Japan. Architect: Akihiko Watanabe/ITO Architects & Engineers Inc.

Figure 14-5.

Sinarmas World Academy students practice traditional Sumi-e painting in the Grade 1-3 Commons.

Campfire Space

The popular author, educator, and PBS commentator David Thornburg proposes four "primordial learning metaphors," which he defines as the Campfire, the Watering Hole, the Cave, and Life. He tells audiences why each of these modalities is important in the overall scheme of learning: Campfires are a way to learn from experts or storytellers; Watering Holes help you learn from peers; Caves are places to learn from yourself; and Life is where you bring it all together by applying what you learn to projects in the real world.

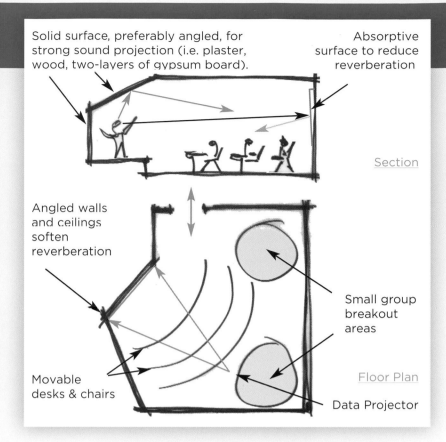

Solid surface, preferably angled, for strong sound projection (i.e. plaster, wood, two-layers of gypsum board).

Absorptive surface to reduce reverberation

Section

Angled walls and ceilings soften reverberation

Small group breakout areas

Movable desks & chairs

Floor Plan

Data Projector

Figure 15-1.
Design Pattern #15: Campfire Space.

Figure 15-2 (bottom left).
Formal Campfire Space at Cristo Rey Jesuit High School, MN.

So how does a school building designed to accommodate the above four modalities look? Some possibilities for Campfire learning can be viewed in Figure 15-1. The Watering Hole, Cave and Life learning modalities are also spelled out as distinct patterns in this book.

These modalities of learning are really the high-end versions of the 20 more defined modalities discussed earlier. A school that is designed to nurture the 20 modalities will also work well with the Thornburg metaphors.

An argument can be made that the Campfire is nothing but a traditional teacher-as-talking-head model of school and so why does it deserve the kind of special attention that the other, 21st century modalities deserve? The answer is there is a place for Campfire learning in today's schools. For a more detailed treatise on this subject, please see the article, "Making Peace with Campfires—Confessions of a Reformed Radical," published by *Education Week* in March 2003. The idea is to celebrate the Campfire and include it as but one of many different ways in which learning will take place in school. There is a need for both formal and informal Campfire spaces in schools.

Campfire Space Characteristics

A good Campfire Space has the following characteristics:

1. A raised section of the room if possible

2. Good sound reflectance behind the speaker's area

3. Desks and chairs that can be arranged in a formal lecture format for more informal "story-telling" mode. See Figure 15-3

4. Data projection screen or large plasma monitor clearly visible to the whole room when the lectures are being delivered electronically or from a distance

5. Provision for the room to be darkened for viewing slide presentations

6. Provision for convenient placement of the presenter's laptop computer with a remote controller and access to sound for multimedia presentations

Figure 15-3.
Campfire Space at Harbor City International School.

7. Access to wireless audio enhancement technology is preferred to give the speaker more freedom to move around the room and speak in a normal voice.

Informal Campfire Space is space that isn't designed purely for Campfire mode, but can easily support a speaker-and-audience situation. Most storytelling arrangements in libraries constitute Informal Campfire Space.

Characteristics of this might include:

- Floor seating, preferably with bean bags or cushions

- A seat at a higher level for the speaker(s)

- Space for the group to sit in a circle

It is possible for Campfire space to also support other modalities, but changing the function of the space needs to be an easy exercise that can be done in the context of a normal school day, using the resources available. See Figure 15-2.

How many Campfires does a school need? A good rule of thumb is for the school community to establish an idea of the average percentage of a student's learning that will ideally happen in a lecture format. (The same rule can be applied to other types of space as well.) This percentage then becomes roughly the percentage of floor space in a school dedicated to Campfire arrangements.

Watering Hole Space

The concept of Watering Holes in schools (Figure 16-1) is alien to the traditional control model of education. Most traditional schools actually discourage social interaction in school as a "distraction" out of fear that when students socialize, they threaten the adult goal of discipline and compliance with adult rules.

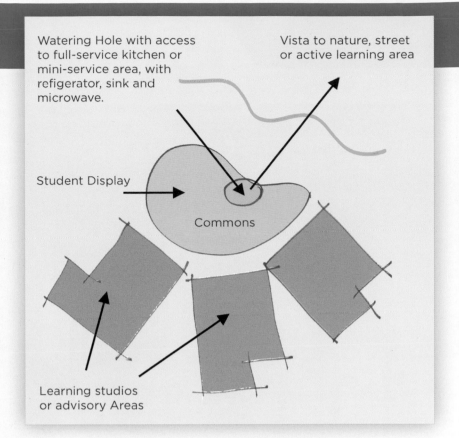

Watering Hole with access to full-service kitchen or mini-service area, with refrigerator, sink and microwave.

Vista to nature, street or active learning area

Student Display

Commons

Learning studios or advisory Areas

Figure 16-1.
Design Pattern #16: Watering Hole Space.

Figure 16-2 (bottom left).
Indoor Watering Holes (such as this at Scotch Oakburn College) are equally important as those outside. They exemplify democratic learning space.

Schools also generally provide little space for students to work together under passive supervision. We now know that social discourse and collaborative learning are critical to the development of well-rounded citizens. These so-called "soft" skills are actually at the top of the list of qualifications for success in almost any profession. Examples of collaborative learning at Harbor City, Henry Park and Scotch Oakburn College show small groups of students at Watering Holes in Figures 16-2, 16-3 and 16-4.

Traditional schools have really only two kinds of space: classrooms, where the power is with the teacher; and corridor and outdoor space, which is rarely furnished adequately for anything other than standing around. There typically is very little space available for students to choose to work or socialize together in. Watering Hole space is able to provide for small group work and socializing. It is important not to label it as 'social space', since this perpetuates the idea that learning only happens under tutelage, and does not embrace the concept of lifelong learning.

This leads to the question—what kind of spaces can we create in schools so that Watering Hole learning flourishes? For starters, we can replace corridors with other kinds of spaces, which permit circulation but also serve the goals of social and emotional development. See Figure 16-5. The Millennium High School in New York City started with a typical corridor plan as in Figure 16-6, but then incorporated some of the healthy design patterns discussed in this book—including the development of many Watering Holes throughout the school. See Figure 16-7.

At Cristo Rey Jesuit High School, Learning-Studio-based Small Learning Communities are each centered around a commons, furnished primarily for Watering Holes (Figure 16-8). This makes for an atmosphere more like a hotel lobby than a typical high school corridor, and students tend to behave accordingly.

The Community Center SLC model (Design Pattern #1) is a more comprehensive embrace of Watering Holes. In this model, there is an implicit invitation to work in that Watering Hole space.

Figure 16-3 (above).
Watering Hole Space at Harbor City International School.

Figure 16-4 (left).
Watering Hole Space at Henry Park Elementary School, Singapore. Architect: CPG Consultants. (Photo Courtesy of Albert Lim KS.)

Figure 16-5.
Watering Hole Space at Millennium High School in New York City, NY. Planner: Fielding Nair International; Architect: HLW International. (Photo Courtesy of Richard Cadan.)

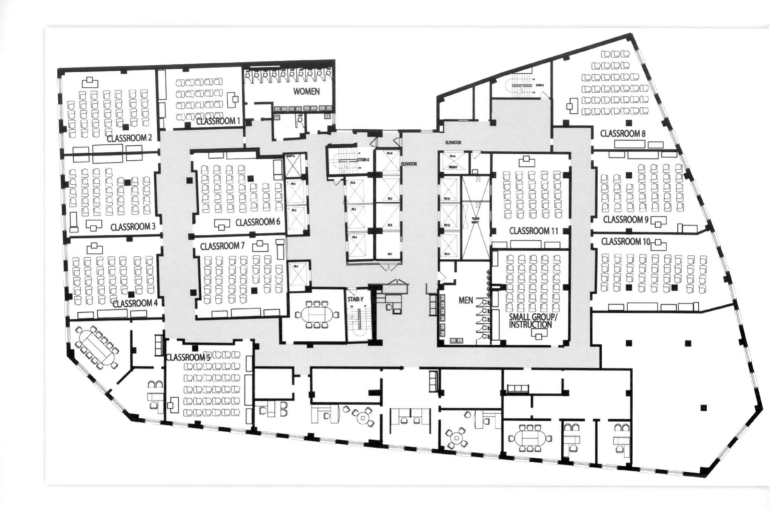

Figure 16-6 (above).
Traditional double-loaded corridor plan first proposed for Millennium High School (not constructed).

Figure 16-7 (right).
Final (constructed) plan for Millennium High School where corridors have been replaced with social learning spaces.

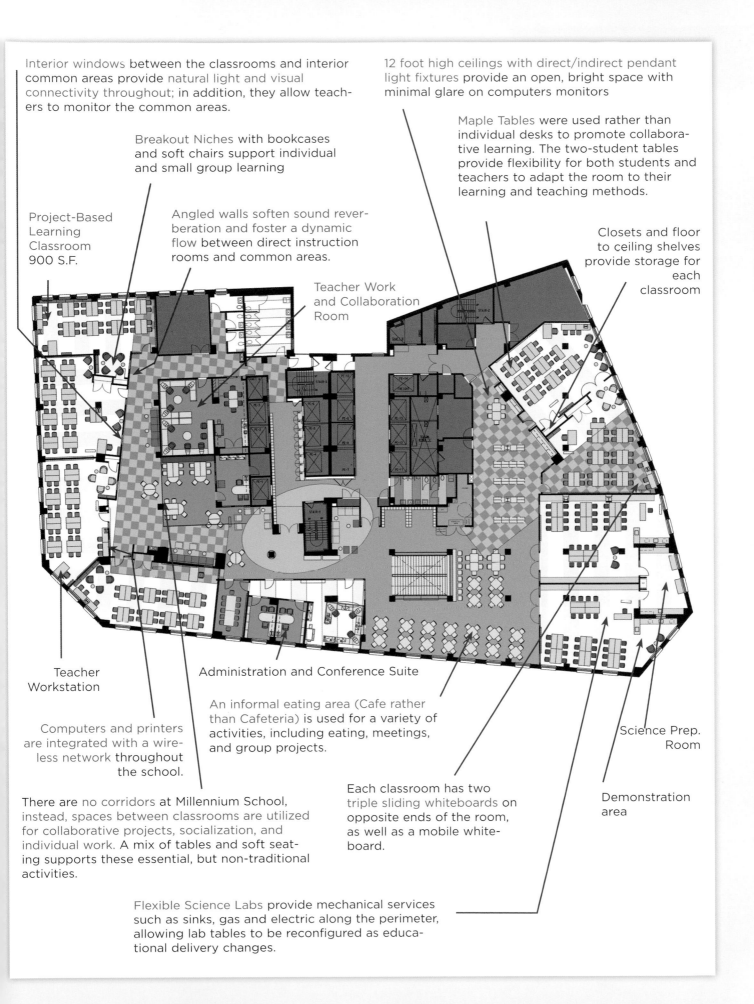

Interior windows between the classrooms and interior common areas provide natural light and visual connectivity throughout; in addition, they allow teachers to monitor the common areas.

Breakout Niches with bookcases and soft chairs support individual and small group learning

Project-Based Learning Classroom 900 S.F.

Angled walls soften sound reverberation and foster a dynamic flow between direct instruction rooms and common areas.

Teacher Work and Collaboration Room

12 foot high ceilings with direct/indirect pendant light fixtures provide an open, bright space with minimal glare on computers monitors

Maple Tables were used rather than individual desks to promote collaborative learning. The two-student tables provide flexibility for both students and teachers to adapt the room to their learning and teaching methods.

Closets and floor to ceiling shelves provide storage for each classroom

Teacher Workstation

Administration and Conference Suite

Computers and printers are integrated with a wireless network throughout the school.

An informal eating area (Cafe rather than Cafeteria) is used for a variety of activities, including eating, meetings, and group projects.

Science Prep. Room

Demonstration area

There are no corridors at Millennium School, instead, spaces between classrooms are utilized for collaborative projects, socialization, and individual work. A mix of tables and soft seating supports these essential, but non-traditional activities.

Each classroom has two triple sliding whiteboards on opposite ends of the room, as well as a mobile whiteboard.

Flexible Science Labs provide mechanical services such as sinks, gas and electric along the perimeter, allowing lab tables to be reconfigured as educational delivery changes.

Figure 16-8.
Cristo Rey Jesuit High School, MN, offers Watering Hole spaces throughout formal and informal learning areas.

Throughout this book, we have stressed the importance of outdoor spaces as logical extensions of the indoor learning experience. This is no different when it comes to Watering Hole spaces. Well-designed outdoor Watering Holes are essential because it gives students an incentive to spend time outside, breathe fresh air and commune with nature. See Figure 16-9.

Figure 16-9.
At Scotch Oakburn College's Middle School's front door, an amphitheater not only provides space for student, teacher or community presentation, but also serves as a Watering Hole for informal, social/emotional learning.

Places for individual study, reflection, quiet reading and creative flow are rare in school.

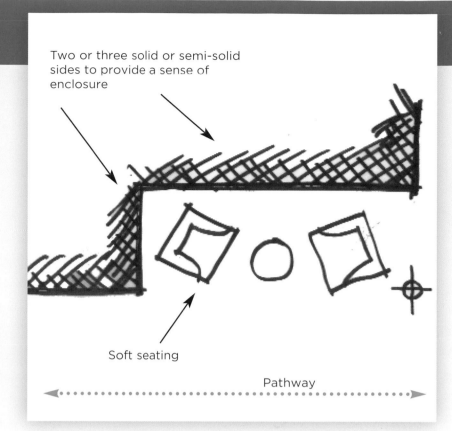

Two or three solid or semi-solid sides to provide a sense of enclosure

Soft seating

Pathway

Figure 17-1.
Design Pattern #17: Cave Space.

Figure 17-2 (bottom left).
Cave Spaces at Canning Vale High School, Perth, Australia. Planner: Prakash Nair; Architect: Spowers/ VITETTA.

It is true that most schools have libraries to encourage reading and independent study, but the problem with libraries is that they are mostly set up according to an adult's view of what a quiet place should be. The very rules that keep a library quiet sometimes make it oppressive for students.

Schools need to explore other areas that can serve as Cave Spaces. See Figure 17-1. Interestingly, it is valuable to understand that not all Cave Space needs to be quiet. An outdoor area by a fountain, benches near a play field or a secluded booth within a café can all be perfectly good Cave Spaces. Even a pull-out niche off a corridor can function as a Cave Space. Since different students are able to concentrate and think more clearly in different kinds of Cave Spaces, the important thing is to provide a variety of nooks and crannies as in Figures 17-2, 17-4 and 17-5 that can serve as Cave Spaces. Interestingly, many formal Cave Spaces such as the Buddha Studio at Duke School can also be very effective since they provide quiet but professionally set up areas for independent study. See Figure 17-3.

Why Cave Space?

Dr. David Thornburg's "Primordial Learning Metaphors" include Campfires, Watering Holes, Caves and Life. In schools, we find that the cave form of learning is never a priority. This is a serious problem because the millions of dollars spent on many new schools will do little to improve educational outcomes if they are built without cave spaces. Particularly in today's chaotic world, children are bombarded by vast amounts of information almost every waking moment. To this you need to add their mobile phones and laptop computers that keep them constantly connected with their peers and with their adult mentors. Even in less developed countries, students are rarely allowed time to be by themselves in school or outside school. This is a serious learning problem because it is in solitude that students assimilate, synthesize and internalize learning so that it becomes knowledge and (sometimes) wisdom. That is the reason why schools have to make every effort to create inviting but supervisable cave spaces where students can check out and take a deep breath, albeit momentarily, from their hectic lives.

Figure 17-3 (above).
Buddha Studio at Duke School serves as a formal
Cave Space.

Figure 17-4 (left).
Cave Space at Tajimi Junior High School, Tajimi-shi,
Gifu, Japan.

Figure 17-5 (right).
Cozy, reflective Cave Space at Galilee Catholic
Learning Community, Aldinga Beach, South
Australia. Russell & Yelland Pty. Ltd. Photography
Courtesy of Michael Bodroghy.

Designing for Multiple Intelligences

Howard Gardner's Multiple Intelligences (MI) theory says that all human beings possess eight "intelligences," though not each of us is necessarily strong in all of them.

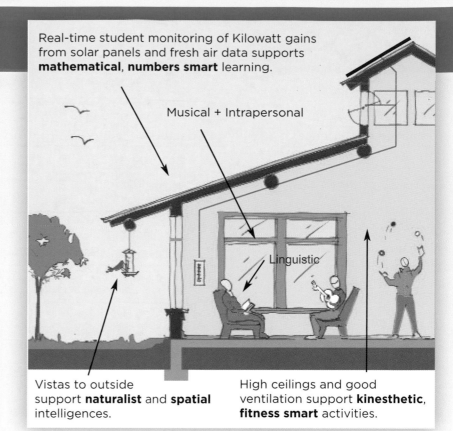

Real-time student monitoring of Kilowatt gains from solar panels and fresh air data supports **mathematical**, **numbers smart** learning.

Musical + Intrapersonal

Linguistic

Vistas to outside support **naturalist** and **spatial** intelligences.

High ceilings and good ventilation support **kinesthetic**, **fitness smart** activities.

Figure 18-1.
Design Pattern #18: Designing for Multiple Intelligences.

Figure 18-2 (bottom left).
Esplanade Library in Singapore: Interpersonal, Intrapersonal and Kinesthetic Intelligences at work.

The eight intelligences are:

1. Linguistic—Word Smart
2. Logical/Mathematical—Numbers Smart
3. Musical—Music Smart
4. Bodily/Kinesthetic—Sports/Fitness Smart
5. Spatial—Picture/3D Smart
6. Naturalist—Nature Smart
7. Interpersonal—Social Smart
8. Intrapersonal—Self Smart

It is important to clarify the issue about the exact number of Multiple Intelligences identified by Howard Gardner, particularly because our chart (Table 18-1) titled *Multiple Intelligences and School Spaces* includes a ninth intelligence called Existential Intelligence or World Smart. Some have said that Howard Gardner had identified this ninth intelligence and there are many references to the Existential Intelligence in writings about MI Theory. When we first included the Existential Intelligence in our chart, we did so with the belief that this important area

of human development could be fostered by the proper design of school spaces. However, we now understand that Howard Gardner himself has not yet endorsed this ninth intelligence. Here's what Tom Hoerr, Head of School, New City School in St. Louis has to say on the subject, *Gardner initially identified seven intelligences and then subsequently named an eighth, the naturalist. I sometimes hear that he has now identified a ninth, the existential intelligence, but that is not the case. A few years ago at New City School, he said that he had not identified the existential intelligence, but that he was still trying to make the determination. In fact, he called it "the eighth and one-half intelligence."*

Even though Gardner developed MI as a theory of the mind and not as an educational intervention strategy, it has naturally entered the realm of education and the classroom. See Figure 18-1. Critics of MI believe that using it in the classroom will prevent ability-based grouping that is associated with higher achievement (for those in the higher ability group). Such criticisms fail to recognize that understanding and applying MI theory in the classroom means to recognize the broad base of talent that is present.

Table 18-1.

Multiple Intelligences and School Spaces. © Fielding Nair International.

	Linguistic	Logical-Mathematical	Musical	Bodily-Kinesthetic	Spatial	Naturalist	Interpersonal	Intrapersonal	Existential
Traditional Classroom	✖	✖					✖		✖
Learning Studio	✖	✖	✖		✖	✖	✖		✖
Advisory Grouping	✖	✖	✖	✖	✖	✖	✖	✖	✖
Cave Space	✖	✖						✖	
Campfire Space	✖	✖							✖
Watering Hole Space	✖	✖					✖		✖
Performance Space			✖	✖	✖		✖		✖
Amphitheater	✖	✖	✖	✖	✖	✖	✖	✖	✖
Café	✖	✖	✖				✖	✖	
Project Studio		✖			✖	✖	✖		
Library	✖	✖	✖		✖	✖	✖	✖	✖
Outdoor Learning Terrace	✖	✖	✖	✖	✖	✖	✖		
Greenhouse		✖		✖	✖	✖	✖		
Distance Learning Center	✖	✖	✖		✖		✖		
Graphic Arts/CADD Lab		✖	✖		✖		✖		✖
Fitness Center			✖	✖	✖		✖	✖	
Playfields				✖	✖	✖	✖	✖	✖
Blackbox Theater			✖	✖	✖		✖		
Entrance Piazza	✖	✖	✖	✖	✖	✖	✖	✖	✖

It does not imply any specific grouping nor does it imply a lack of rigor or a watered-down curriculum. If anything, it fosters a deeper understanding of what is being learned and encourages a more rigorous and holistic examination of the subject.

MI theory, when properly applied in school, provides students with the opportunity to become engaged in subjects that may not otherwise have held their interest. It can help students learn and strengthen an area of intelligence in which they are weak by supplementing their experience with another intelligence area in which they are strong.

For example, a student that may have a hard time learning a subject in a traditional classroom setting (using his or her cognitive intelligence) may be able to learn the same thing more effectively through performance (bodily–kinesthetic/interpersonal/musical intelligences). See Figure 18-3.

But we should also remember that as humans, we tend to naturally favor our strongest intelligences—often at the expense of developing our other intelligences. This imbalance can hurt us in life where most of the intelligences have value. A balanced educational program will allow students to fully sharpen the "favored" intelligences, as well

Figure 18-3.
Performance space for Musical and Kinesthetic Intelligences at Hip-Hop High.

as encourage exploration of the world utilizing their other intelligences.

When it comes to the design of spaces, we are more likely to create interesting and exciting learning environments when we try to accommodate as many of the intelligences as possible. See Figure 18-2 and 18-4.

The New City School in St. Louis, Missouri, one of the MI pioneers in the U.S., where a library addition was recently built, is a model of how MI can be respected, even when it comes to elements that have traditionally been very one-dimensional. See Figure 18-5. The New City library is special because it recognizes the core mission of the space—designed to encourage reading and research—but has found ways to go beyond the linguistic and logical/mathematical intelligences of traditional libraries.

As we discussed earlier, different school spaces that nurture MI are configured in the chart "Multiple Intelligences and

Figure 18-4.
Spaces to nurture Interpersonal Intelligence, Yeshiva Elementary School in Milwaukee, WI. Design Architect: Randall Fielding, Fielding Nair International; Project Architect: Haag Muller. (Photo Courtesy of Mark Koerner.)

School Spaces." This chart (Table 18-1) demonstrates how some learning environments, like the Learning Studio, are superior from an MI standpoint to a traditional classroom. It is interesting to note that the Advisory Grouping and the Amphitheater are two physical settings in which all nine intelligences can be nurtured. The library (if properly designed) and an outdoor learning terrace and piazza are also good from an MI standpoint because they can accommodate up to eight intelligences. The Learning Studio comes next with seven intelligences and the other, more specialized areas, predictably, are less flexible and therefore, cater specifically to particular intelligences.

Tailored to match the specific program of spaces in any given school, the chart (Table 18-1) can be a valuable tool to measure the design's effectiveness from an MI perspective. It will allow changes early in the design process to increase the learning value of each space by making it serve as many of the intelligences as possible.

Figure 18-5.

New City Library: Multiple Intelligences theory in action. Architect: HKW Architects.

Daylight and Solar Energy

Of all the elements that make up a high performance school, none has greater impact on the quality of learning than daylight. See Figure 19-1.

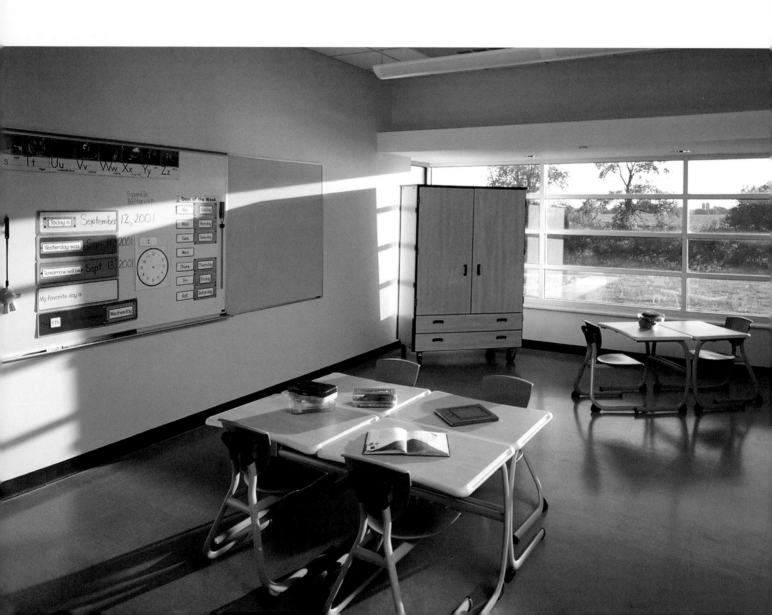

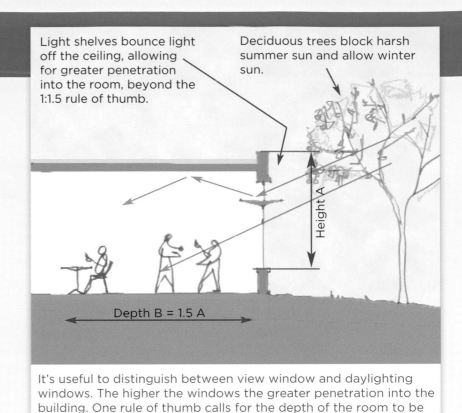

Light shelves bounce light off the ceiling, allowing for greater penetration into the room, beyond the 1:1.5 rule of thumb.

Deciduous trees block harsh summer sun and allow winter sun.

Height A

Depth B = 1.5 A

It's useful to distinguish between view window and daylighting windows. The higher the windows the greater penetration into the building. One rule of thumb calls for the depth of the room to be 1.5 X the height of the window.

Figure 19-1.
Design Pattern #19: Daylighting.

Figure 19-2 (bottom left).
Day-lit classroom with moveable storage at Harold G. Fearn Elementary School, Aurora, IL. Architect: Perkins+Will. (Photo Courtesy of Greg Murphey.)

Daylight can be introduced into school buildings in many ways—including windows, skylights and light shelves. See also Figure 19-3. Sometimes, entire outside walls can disappear through the use of overhead doors and moveable panels so that daylight can wash into interior spaces.

Daylight is important because there are direct connections between our physiological well-being as humans and the amount of daylight we get. It is vital that children who are trapped in school buildings for most of the day spend significant time in rooms with natural daylight. This can be accomplished by good design as with the classrooms at the Harold G. Fearn Elementary School by Perkins+Will, which are bright, cheerful and washed with daylight. See Figure 19-2. Often teachers will close blinds during significant parts of the day to avoid glare but many such rooms end up being permanently shut off from having any natural light at all. One solution is to bring in daylight into spaces such as commons areas through the use of diffused and glare-free skylights such as those utilized at the Duke School. This system, when combined with light sensors attached to the lighting fixtures, will not only create a warm, healthy environment, but also result in a substantial reduction in energy consumption. See Figure 19-4.

Daylight is also important because, used intelligently, it can substantially reduce the energy load on buildings. This applies both to the electrical and heating load of a given building.

Beyond its obvious benefit as a source of light, daylight can also meet some of the building's energy needs. While sunlight-based systems (photo voltaics) are not yet fully cost-effective to heat and cool the whole building, they do work very well for smaller applications such as providing domestic hot water.

Beyond this, they are valuable because of their environmental friendliness and the great potential they have to teach students about energy conservation and utilization. See Figure 19-5.

To get the most value from daylight, it is important to properly "manage" it with shading devices, thoughtfully located trees and other vegetation, and by properly orienting the building on site. Light sensors on windows can control blinds automatically for glare reduction. See Figure 19-6.

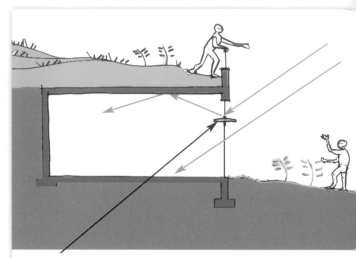

Figure 19-3 (right).
Design Pattern #19a: Green Roof and Light Shelf.

Figure 19-4 (bottom).
Diffused Daylight from skylights means this commons area at the Duke School is always bright, cheerful, healthy and, through the use of light sensors, it also saves energy by turning off the electric lights automatically when not needed.

A light shelf extends light penetration by reflecting light off of the ceiling.

A green roof increases the percentage of natural vistas, while providing effective insulation and reduced energy costs.

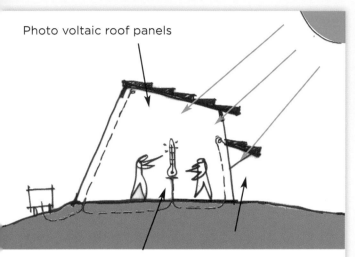

Photo voltaic roof panels

Voltage meter allows students to monitor energy transferred from photo voltaic cells.

Rather than hiding photo voltaic cells, they may be placed in highly visible locations, such as on an entry canopy, making the building a 3-dimensional text book.

Figure 19-5 (left).
Design Pattern #19b: Energy from the Sun.

Figure 19-6 (bottom).
Natural Daylighting at Hosmarinpuisto School, Espoo, Finland.

Natural Ventilation

School building design needs to maximize access to natural ventilation. Like daylight, natural air contributes to a healthy environment. See Figure 20-1. It can alleviate or eliminate some of the more serious problems associated with spending excessive amounts of time in conditioned spaces.

Figure 20-1.
Design Pattern #20: Natural Ventilation.

Figure 20-2 (bottom left).
This image of an indoor-outdoor cafe in Malaysia shows how schools can also take advantage of well-designed transition areas in warmer climates to provide naturally ventilated high-quality and less expensive learning environments.

Figure 20-3 (bottom right).
Section showing Daylighting and Natural Ventilation at Clackamas High School, OR. Architect: Boora Architects.

Low winter sun provides daylight and passive solar heat.

Electricity generated by wind turbine powers heat pump fan.

Low intake window and high ventilation windows take advantage of "stack effect".

Water body placed in front of prevailing summer breeze provides natural cooling.

Geo Thermal Loop provides both heating and cooling.

Naturally ventilated buildings reduce the amount of toxins in the air that are released by a variety of building products. Natural ventilation can also prevent the formation of mold which can cause severe health problems, such as Sick Building Syndrome.

There are two ways to ensure that buildings have adequate natural ventilation. The first way is to develop mechanical systems that have the capacity to draw in a significant amount of outside air into the building while maintaining a high ratio of fresh air to reconditioned air as shown in Figure 20-2. In fact, building codes spell out the amount of fresh air that is necessary to maintain a healthy indoor environment. The second method is to use natural air-flow patterns to circulate fresh air within the building. This system usually supplements mechanical systems that are in place but, on nice days, natural ventilation can take most of the load off the mechanical system and save energy costs.

Another reason for natural ventilation is that it gives the users greater power over the quality of the air they breathe. Beyond the measurable benefits noted above, there is a value to giving occupants of the building the ability to open windows and let in natural air. It provides a sense of connectedness to the outdoors that the best mechanically ventilated building cannot provide.

Opening windows can be controlled by thermostat, so that when the outside temperature becomes pleasant, the windows open automatically, and the heating/cooling system turns off.

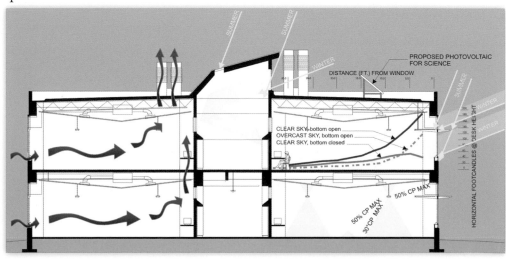

Learning, Lighting and Color[1]

Uniform illumination levels in the classroom and focused brightness on the "teaching wall" made good sense for students in Henry Ford's era. If you were training to take your place on the assembly line, you needed to focus on the work at hand, but the future no longer belongs to students who look only straight ahead.

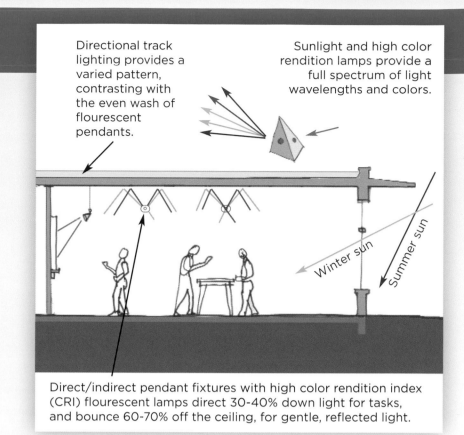

Directional track lighting provides a varied pattern, contrasting with the even wash of flourescent pendants.

Sunlight and high color rendition lamps provide a full spectrum of light wavelengths and colors.

Winter sun

Summer sun

Direct/indirect pendant fixtures with high color rendition index (CRI) flourescent lamps direct 30-40% down light for tasks, and bounce 60-70% off the ceiling, for gentle, reflected light.

Figure 21-1 (inset).
Design Pattern #21: Lighting, Learning and Color.

Figure 21-2.
These pendant lighting fixtures at the Duke School are equipped with light sensors that turn off the lights when there is ample daylight.

Today's schools need to be places where students are offered a wide variety of learning options that simulate the real conditions they will encounter in the world outside. Creating a 21st century environment for learning whose ambiance is very different from the institutional character of the traditional school requires a thoughtful approach to color and lighting as discussed in this chapter.

Vistas, Movement, and Lighting Design Principles

It's a natural reflex to look up from a task frequently, and refocus on an element in the distance. People often do this unconsciously. For example, if you observe people at work in a library or office you will see them shifting their gaze toward something in the distance. In fact, they are resting their eyes by changing their visual focal length—and thereby stretching tired eye muscles.

Most humans also instinctively move towards light and color (unless we are frightened, and in a flight state). Designers can take advantage of these natural reflexes to look up and out and towards light by creating vistas to define and order movement, by leading first the eye and then the body through space.

Movement is a stimulus for learning, but paths that are confusing or counter-intuitive don't make us feel secure enough to learn at our best. Designers can use movement as a positive design generator by choreographing scenarios in advance. Imagine that you are entering a campus or school building. What do you see? Where is your eye drawn to? If a visual element at the far corner from a visitor's starting point is highlighted, a person will be attracted to move towards it. The visual destination element may be a sculptural form, taller than the elements around it, or it could be a wall with a brighter color, and a higher level of illumination.

[1] - Co-published in German and English by *PLD*—the official magazine of the ELDA (European Lighting Designers' Association) and the IALD (International Association of Lighting Designers). http://www.pldplus.com, "Learning, Lighting and Color: Lighting Design for Schools and Universities in the 21st Century," Randall Fielding, 2006 - and by Edutopia. "What They See Is What We Get: Ten myths about lighting and color in schools," Randall Fielding, March 2006..

Full-Spectrum Lighting

Lighting designers often wrinkle their noses when someone mentions full-spectrum lighting—thinking of the hyped commercial claims for "miracle lights." There is not a good consensus on the definition of a full-spectrum lamp, or on its clinical benefits.

The desire for a broad spectrum of light and color is consistent with a more holistic curriculum—one that takes into account a variety of learning styles and modalities. We all learn differently and at different times. We need a variety of lighting levels and qualities and colors of light. It's natural to want lighting that most closely matches the full spectrum of daylight. The pattern for full spectrum lighting is one example of how this is applied in a learning studio. See Figure 21-1. The following examples of 21st century school design patterns illustrate how these lighting design principles apply.

Welcoming Entry

It's important for a school or university to have a signature—a unique presence in the landscape or cityscape and community. Learners that feel a sense of connection and personal identification with a small learning community (SLC) attain higher test scores and have a significantly greater graduation rate. Research demonstrates that "small" is defined as 150 students or less. A recent study by Albuquerque Public Schools demonstrates conclusively that the positive effects of 120-student academies are completely lost when the academies grow to 180.

Since most schools and universities accommodate more than 150 students, one way to leverage the positive effects of small learning communities is to break down the scale of the environment into smaller buildings or clusters of spaces. The entry to each SLC can be individualized, reinforcing its unique identity. Lighting plays an important role in creating this identity.

The entry area includes a series of interconnected spaces, each warranting a different approach to lighting. The signature element and student display area should be highlighted. For display areas, track fixtures are all good options, with wall wash, linear, directional and low voltage lights. In the office and community space, a mix of direct/indirect pendants with directional fixtures in selected areas usually makes sense.

The principles of movement and lighting apply to all of the spaces connected to the entry way itself. For example, the wall opposite the entry door to the community space might have a deeper color and a large mural reflecting unique qualities of the community. Directional lighting on the mural would highlight it with a high illumination level. The rest of the room might utilize direct/indirect pendants, with a distribution of 60% uplight and 40% downlight.

Figure 21-3.
Pendant lighting fixtures at Harbor City International High School.

Science Lab Areas

Science education at its best takes advantage of all of our senses—it's at once analytical, mathematical, collaborative and kinesthetic. The pattern for science and life skills, such as student interaction and collaboration, supports all of these modalities. One learning community in Bridgehampton, NY used this pattern as a basis for all of its learning spaces, including arts and humanities. The traditional departmental separation between "soft" humanities subjects and "hard" sciences reinforces, in a negative sense, the 19th and 20th century schism between analytical and synthetic thinking. Conversely the pattern shown here brings analytical, intuitive, and kinesthetic strengths together to foster innovation and conceptual thinking.

The lighting should vary to reflect the character of each space. The soft seating in the research and development (R&D) think tank might include low voltage pendants for soft, ambient light. The walls of the same space would benefit from directional track or linear fluorescents to highlight "tech art" and student work on the walls. Direct/indirect pendant fixtures in the active lab space might reverse the percentage of up and downlight used in humanities spaces, with 60% or 70% downlight versus 40%.

Learning from the Past

Before developing new patterns for learning and design in the future, it's useful to look back and avoid the mistakes of the past. Many myths about lighting and color need to be dispelled.

Seven Myths about Lighting and Color in Educational Architecture

Myth #1: Uniform brightness level: Many educational "specs" and building codes call for a uniform brightness of 55 foot candles in academic spaces. However, in 20 years of educational architecture, we have never been "written up" for varying the lighting levels. As discussed in the beginning of this chapter, uniform illumination makes more sense for assembly line training. For the holistic thinkers of the 21st century, however, it's a concept that has passed its time. Alternatively, 55 foot candles can light the center of the room, with lower illumination in a niche or bay that serves as a breakout space, and higher illumination on display walls. See Figures 21-2 and 21-3.

Myth #2: Primary colors for children: Often the strategy is expressed that brightly lit, primary colors are the best environments for young children. This is not born out by any reputable research. In fact, experience has shown that children are wonderfully sensitive and responsive to nuances in both lighting and color. For example, children are particularly attuned to the colors of nature and human skin tones, and yet these are completely out of the primary range. Primaries can be harsh—use them sparingly.

Myth #3: Red incites aggression, green is calming: The research indicating that the color red incites aggression, green is calming and yellow stimulates the intellect is simplistic and outdated. Hundreds, if not thousands, of schools, hospitals and prisons were painted light green (thought to induce calm) in the middle of the 20th century, with the result that this perfectly good color family was tainted as an "institutional kiss of death" by the 1980s and 90s. All colors have a place for learners of all ages, when used thoughtfully. A good application depends on the cultural and climatic context, available resources and lighting.

It's a good idea to use a larger percentage of ceiling and wall surfaces with a higher Light Reflectance Value (LRV), in order to boost lighting efficiency. (Lighting designers can reduce the number of fixtures by as much as 25% by taking the LRV of adjacent surfaces into account.) Efficiency, however, is not a good reason to use exclusively light colors. Utilizing more saturated accent colors in selected areas is more important for providing a varied, stimulating learning environment.

Figure 21-4.

Daylit gymnasium at Cristo Rey Jesuit High School. For a more dramatic example of a daylit gymnasium, see Figure 22-4, the glass-walled gymnasium at Colegio Altamira High School.

Myth #4: Neutral colors are best: A common myth is that the best palette for learning environments is comprised of neutral colors, because it allows the students and teacher to become the focus, rather than the architecture. This is the same reasoning that was used in the 1960s and '70s to justify the proliferation of sterile glass, steel and aluminum boxes in cities around the world. The thought was that flexible, rationally engineered buildings could house anything with equal efficiency, downplaying monumental architecture and reinforcing "humanity" instead. This strategy of neutral design backfired and resulted in a period of architectural history often considered soulless.

Architects may proclaim proudly that they have specified six different shades of white in a school building, only to find that the architects are the only ones who notice any distinction between the shades of white! Research shows that learning benefits from a stimulus-rich environment, which is not supported by a palette that is dominated by gray, beige, white or off white; this applies to both building interiors and exteriors. There is rarely a good reason to take a neutral approach with educational architecture.

Myth #5: It's best to use all the same lamps: Such uniformity has nothing to do with how we learn, but rather what's easiest to manage. This myth only eases the burden on maintenance people who will want to stock a single lamp type. This is like forcing all students to sit still on hard plastic chairs and stare straight ahead, listening to the same thing at the same time. Businesses can't compete using this kind of approach—if businesses don't respond to what consumers want, competitors will win the business. Learning organizations are becoming more like businesses; the successful ones are focusing on the educational consumer, not on their own convenience. Stock a variety of lamp types, and prioritize the needs of the learner.

Myth #6: It's best not to use natural light in gymnasiums: It is often assumed that natural light is difficult to control, but natural light is perhaps the single-most important element in the learning environment. See Figure 21-4. Research shows that in day-lit classrooms math scores improve by 20% and verbal scores by 22%. Eliminating natural light in gymnasiums because it's difficult to control glare is a lazy approach to design. Using north light, filtered light, and adjustable lighting control devices are just a few ways to utilize natural light in a competitive athletic environment. While it's impossible to predict all of the ways that spaces will be used in a vibrant school or university over time, insure that a majority of those spaces are illuminated by daylight.

Myth #7: Performance spaces should not have any windows: This myth is based on the assumption that it's important to control the lighting. There are many expensive, windowless black boxes with proud facility owners. After hundreds of hours with drama, dance and music performers, our experience is that performers would prefer spaces that more closely resemble artists' lofts with lots of light and views of the city, landscape, or campus green. The big picture idea with a black box theater is about a space that is adaptable, and less structured than a traditionally rigged theater, with a fly space, heavy curtain, and proscenium stage. At a high school in New York, the board—mostly comprised of professional theater people—asked for a black box approach, because they felt that it challenged students to think more creatively than a fully rigged theater. A better term for black box might be a white box—a kind of "Tabula Rasa"—a blank canvas for students to design, rather than have the structure of the theater itself dictate the creative approach. In a similar manner, designers do not need to rigidly dictate in advance how theater students will light the "house." It is better to provide them with choices, including an option for natural light and transparent surfaces that allow for interconnectivity among performance spaces, social spaces, and learning areas.

Sustainable Elements and Building as 3-D Textbook

Today, the term "High Performance" is a buzzword in school design—and rightly so. High performance refers both to the performance of the building itself, as well as to those who live and work in buildings.

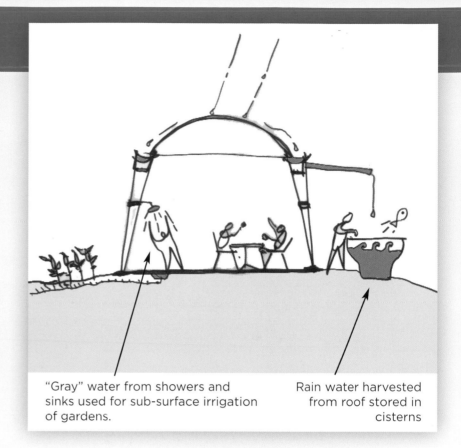

Figure 22-1.
Design Pattern #22: Sustainable Elements and Building as 3-D Textbook.

Figure 22-2 (bottom left).
The water habitat demonstrates the harvesting and use of rainwater at the school site. Roy Lee Walker Elementary School, McKinney, Texas. Architect: SHW Group, Inc.; Sustainable Design Consultant: Innovative Design. (Photo Courtesy of Jim Wilson.)

"Gray" water from showers and sinks used for sub-surface irrigation of gardens.

Rain water harvested from roof stored in cisterns

Sustainable architecture is one of the key underpinnings of high performance design in several ways:

1. It involves a thoughtful approach that tries to minimize the disruption of a site's natural features.

2. It taps nature's energy sources from the earth, wind and sun to minimize the consumption of fossil fuels.

3. It utilizes indigenous materials—materials with high recyclable content and materials that do not cause health problems from the emission of toxic vapors.

4. Sustainable design is also about minimizing the consumption of water within the building, capturing and utilizing rainwater, and minimizing erosion and water runoff from the site.

But high performance design can also be seen on a larger scale—it is about seeing the school itself as part of a larger social "eco-system" and connecting it more closely to its community—as a way to complement the community's resources and also reduce the amount of infrastructure that may have to be developed on a given site by sharing existing community facilities. (See Design Pattern #24—"Connected to the Community.")

In a school setting, sustainable design becomes an excellent teaching tool. It can become a dynamic model to teach architecture, engineering, construction, and environmental science in harmony with nature. See Figure 22-1.

Even though sustainable design is as important as one might imagine, it does not always capture the imaginations of school communities. Design Patterns can be useful here because they can make this subject more intuitively understandable, and school stakeholders can become more personally connected to the goals of high performance design.

Some examples of Design Patterns that demonstrate sustainable principles have already been shown: Figure 12-1 (*Indoor–Outdoor Connection*), Figures 19-3 and 19-5 (*Lighting*) and Figure 20-1 (*Natural Ventilation*). In this section, additional important designs are illustrated.

Figure 22-3 deals with parking—a very important consideration in school planning everywhere. The parking pattern shows how a necessary parking lot that needs to be on site can be developed so that the cars are out of sight from within the building. With berms, garden walls, steps, plantings or a combination of these elements, the building occupants can still relate to nature instead of parked cars.

The value of sustainable architecture as a teaching tool should not be underestimated. Sustainable architecture is often one where building systems can be readily apparent as in the gymnasium of Colegio Altamira High School in Penalolen, Chile. See Figure 22-4. Transparent architecture and engineering systems are ideal in a learning setting because they can engage students' imaginations and spur learning about buildings as 3-dimensional textbooks.

While most schools designed today make at least some token gesture toward sustainability, there are few buildings designed from the ground up as sustainable "green" schools. The Roy Lee Walker Elementary School in McKinney, Texas is a notable exception. It was recognized by the American Institute of Architects as one of the top ten "Most Environmentally Responsible Design Projects" in the nation. See Figures 22-2 and 22-5. Roberta Furger, writing for the September/October 2004 issue of *Edutopia* magazine had this to say about the school:

> Instead of the concrete-and-glass sameness that passes for modern educational design, six large stone cisterns squat near the building, each brimming with nearly 10,000 gallons of rainwater that have rolled from the school's roof during the region's window-rattling thunderstorms. Nearby, a 30-foot windmill twirls languidly in the breeze, powering a filtering system that removes sediment from the collected water, which is used to irrigate the buffalo grass and other native vegetation that fill the grounds. Slanted solar panels poke up from the roof of the single-story building, and inside, classrooms are lit not with the cold gray glare of fluorescent lights but with the warmth of natural sunlight.

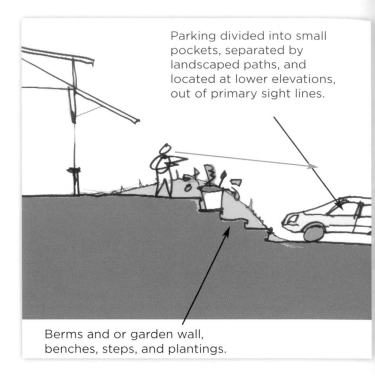

Parking divided into small pockets, separated by landscaped paths, and located at lower elevations, out of primary sight lines.

Berms and or garden wall, benches, steps, and plantings.

Figure 22-3 (above).
Design Pattern #22a: Cars Out Of Sight.

Figure 22-4 (top right).
With the structure fully articulated, this gymnasium is an excellent illustration of the term, "Building as a 3-D Textbook". Colegio Altamira High School, Penalolen, Chile. Architect: Mathias Klotz.

Figure 22-5 (bottom right).
Front exterior view of Roy Lee Walker Elementary School, McKinney, Texas. Architect: SHW Group, Inc.; Sustainable Design Consultant: Innovative Design. (Photo Courtesy of Jim Wilson.)

Local Signature

We touched upon the importance of a Local Signature in discussing Design Pattern #2—"Welcoming Entry." In thematically focused schools, the signature element is more easily defined because it can be associated with the school's theme—environmental science, music, art, technology, etc. All schools have something about them that is special and unique, however, and the architecture should preferably showcase this.

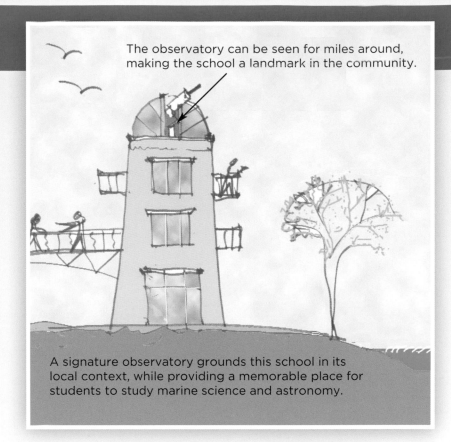

The observatory can be seen for miles around, making the school a landmark in the community.

A signature observatory grounds this school in its local context, while providing a memorable place for students to study marine science and astronomy.

Figure 23-1.
Design Pattern #23: Local Signature, Goa International School.

Figure 23-2 (bottom left).
Signature architecture at Canning Vale Community College in Perth, Western Australia.

In some cases, the architecture of the school can itself become its signature element. The sculptural quality of the architecture sets the Canning Vale Community College in Western Australia (Figure 23-2 and Figure 23-3) apart from all the other buildings in the community and gives the school a unique identity or "signature."

A school's signature element could also be a free-standing sculpture or a piece of artwork that is incorporated into the building architecture: a fountain, a garden, a special place for student-built projects, or some piece of history representative of the site on where the school is located.

Sometimes the school's signature can be a compelling icon that defines a whole community. At the Goa International School in India, situated along the ocean, the team created an "observatory" tower that will be visible from across the bay. The lighthouse is, in fact, a multilevel learning place for oceanography and astronomy (Figure 23-1 and Figure 23-5). The observatory will not only be architecturally significant—giving the school its signature image—it will also contain Learning Studios to teach oceanography and astronomy. The upper level will house a powerful telescope to study the stars.

While many signature elements are permanent, that is not always the case. At a small school in Bridgehampton, young children built a "tepee" in their nature garden using local materials, shown in Figure 23-4. Students, staff and parents felt proud of this temporary structure that immediately became an identifying, signature element.

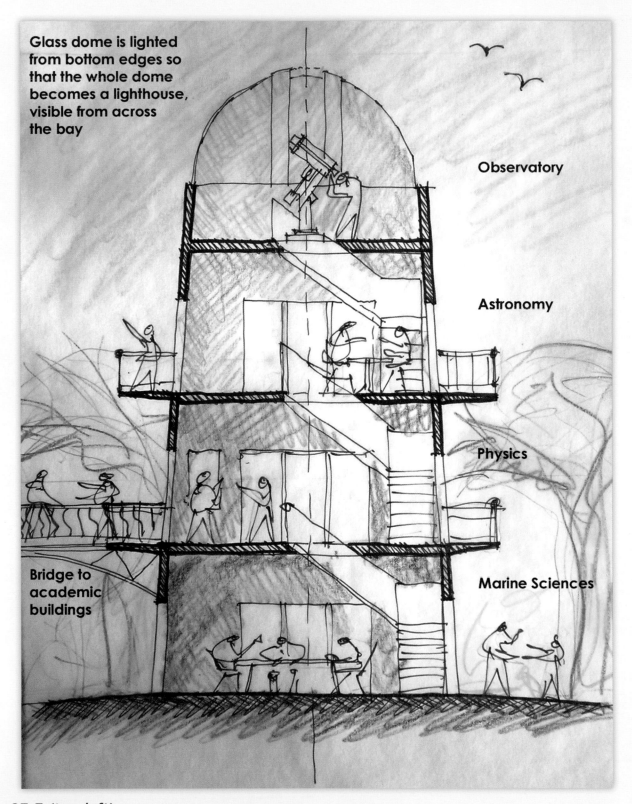

Glass dome is lighted from bottom edges so that the whole dome becomes a lighthouse, visible from across the bay

Observatory

Astronomy

Physics

Marine Sciences

Bridge to academic buildings

Figure 23-3 (top left).
Signature architecture at Canning Vale Community College.

Figure 23-4 (bottom left).
Student-built tepee at the Morriss Center School, Bridgehampton, NY. High School Master Planners and Architect: Helpern Architects with Fielding Nair International.

Figure 23-5 (above).
Sketch of the Goa International School observatory whose theme is "From the Sea to the Sky." Includes observatory, science libraries, Student Display areas.

Connected to the Community

There are three separate aspects that make a school a community school. The first is its location in a place that is close to the heart of its community. The second are the ties the school makes to community businesses, organizations, industries and recreational amenities as a way to extend the school's learning potential beyond its own four walls. See Figure 24-1. The third is the way the school itself is designed to be a welcoming place for the community—extending the so-called school day so that the facilities are open very early in the morning and late into the evening.

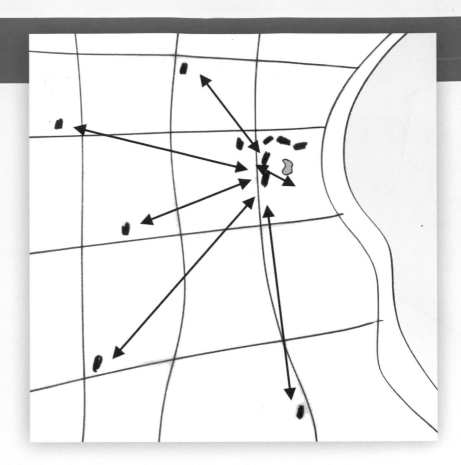

Figure 24-1.

Design Pattern #24: Connected to the Community. Ecology is about more than saving energy—it's about a web of interrelated relationships. Partnerships and shared facilities are not only cost-efficient, they are a lesson in global citizenship.

Figure 24-2 (bottom left).

Connected to the Community. West Metro Education Program (WMEP) Interdistrict Downtown School, Minneapolis, MN. Architect: Cuningham Group Architecture, P.A. (Photo Courtesy of Peter Kerze.)

One school that is very successful at utilizing a variety of community resources in its vicinity is the Interdistrict Downtown School in Minneapolis, MN. The advantage of this system is that the school itself can be built without many of the amenities that would be needed if all the services had to be provided under one roof.

According to a *New Schools Better Neighborhoods* study, the $14.2 million, state-funded Interdistrict Downtown School (IDDS), built atop a city-owned, underground parking ramp, with neighbors that include an historic theater, a university, a church and a photo production house, has formed partnerships with the University of St. Thomas, MacPhail Center for the Arts, Orchestra Hall, Minneapolis Downtown Library, Hennepin County Government Center, Downtown YMCA, Loring Park, the historic Orpheum Theatre and numerous downtown Minneapolis businesses. See Figure 24-2.

Another good example of a school that takes full advantage of its downtown location is the Harbor City International School in Duluth, MN, as shown in Figure 24-3. This charter school has partnerships with the local YMCA, the public library, City Theater and the Fresh Water Aquarium.

When schools are built with a host of specialized amenities because there aren't enough of them in the neighborhood for the students, then it is vital that as many of these amenities as possible become shared community resources. In Des Moines, Iowa the idea of schools becoming true community centers is supported by keeping the buildings open late into the evening and on weekends so that community residents can utilize them—for everything from adult education programs to recreational activities such as music, dance and community theater. In such cases, it is important to separate the community-use facilities from parts of the school that belong exclusively to the students, not only to keep the student areas secure, but also to improve the efficiency of building management and energy consumption.

Site Design for Community

David Engwicht refers to most urban design as being fundamentalist. By this, he means that we view each part of our urban landscape as being useful for one particular function. With that mindset we might say that homes are for living, workplaces are for working, schools are for learning, shops are for buying and roads are for transport.

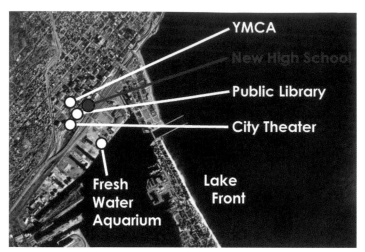

Figure 24-3.
Connected to the Community. Harbor City International School, Duluth, MN.

We can see that the definitions of these things—learning, living, buying, working, transport—are often interpreted narrowly as well, with the attitudes that streets are for cars and schools are for classes.

A good rule of thumb for creating community-friendly spaces is to use human beings, not cars or classes, as the primary unit of design. See Figure 24-4. These human beings may use cars, or take part in classes, but to design so rigidly that space can only be used by people when they're in cars, or part of a class, significantly narrows the scope available for safety and appeal of other ways of being. A road designed only with cars in mind becomes unsafe for cyclists or pedestrians, because the traffic travels too fast, and all of its parts are car-sized—humans are squashed out. A school designed as a series of classrooms reduces opportunity for student-directed learning because it is difficult to passively supervise.

All of the patterns contained in this book combine together to help to create community, most significantly because they are ergonomic: supportive of human beings and all our modes of learning. Making whole school sites to create community introduces a few more issues that we will address here.

Firstly, creating authentic learning opportunities necessarily involves leading the school outside, and the wider community inside. This means taking advantage of local public facilities, businesses, organizations and other schools. Cristo Rey Jesuit High School (MN) and The Met School (RI) both embrace this concept through use of community-based internships that form 20-40% of each student's learning program. Caroline Springs (Melbourne, Australia) is home to four co-located schools, public and private, that share key resources. Western Heights College (Geelong, Australia) is co-located with a community center, a skate park and sporting clubs, all of which are able to be accessed by the school community and vice-versa.

This permeation of opportunities can be supported through site design that embraces the same kinds of principles that as those behind the Community Center Model Small Learning Community.

1. Small Learning Communities

2. Human-scaled site entrance

3. Entrance that blends with most major parts of surrounding community (e.g. shops)

4. Parking away from sight-lines

5. Driveways minimal, paved and narrow to engender a sense of the unexpected (thus making drivers more alert and cautious)

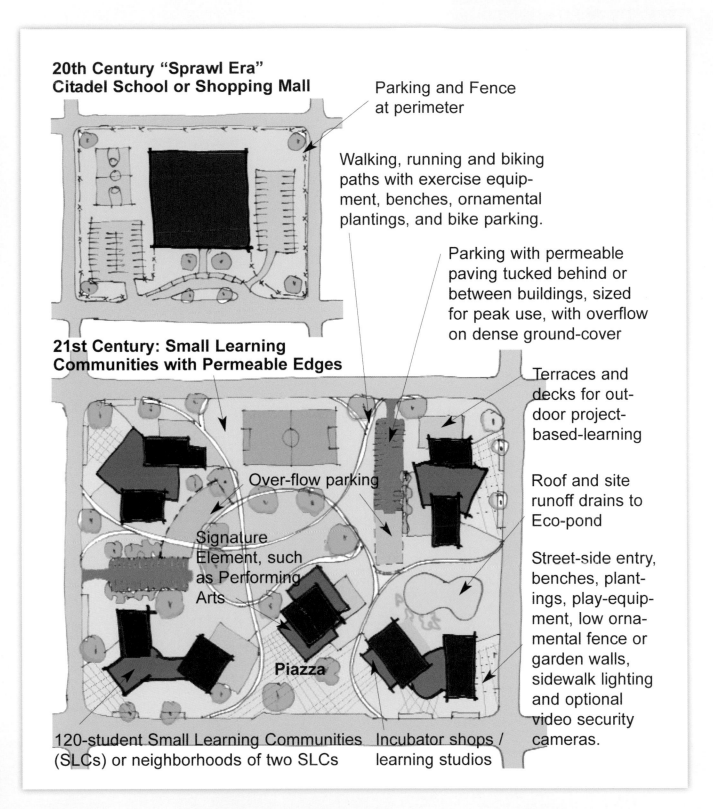

20th Century "Sprawl Era" Citadel School or Shopping Mall

Parking and Fence at perimeter

Walking, running and biking paths with exercise equipment, benches, ornamental plantings, and bike parking.

Parking with permeable paving tucked behind or between buildings, sized for peak use, with overflow on dense ground-cover

21st Century: Small Learning Communities with Permeable Edges

Terraces and decks for outdoor project-based-learning

Over-flow parking

Roof and site runoff drains to Eco-pond

Signature Element, such as Performing Arts

Street-side entry, benches, plantings, play-equipment, low ornamental fence or garden walls, sidewalk lighting and optional video security cameras.

Piazza

120-student Small Learning Communities (SLCs) or neighborhoods of two SLCs

Incubator shops / learning studios

Figure 24-4.
Design Pattern #24a: Site Design for Community.

Home-like Bathrooms

The design of bathrooms in a traditional school, like the school itself, is seriously flawed, yet little attention is paid to this problem.

visible short hallway with no activities deters students from gathering in bathrooms and helps prevent bullying and other antisocial activities

transparent door leading from small learning community increases safety in bathrooms

Figure 25-1.
Design Pattern #25: Home-like Bathrooms.

Figure 25-2 (bottom left).
Passive Supervision in the Bathrooms at St. Aloysius High School in Tasmania, Australia. (Photo Courtesy of Dr. Stephen Heppell.)

Discussions about bathroom design, if it is discussed at all, seem mostly to be a matter of numbers—and even these are often stipulated by building code in many countries. As for location, designers seem less interested in convenience for students and more interested in saving on plumbing costs by creating fewer but larger bathrooms. We have even seen designs where there is a so-called "bathroom block" compelling all students in the school to travel to one remote location to use it.

In many schools, cramped, dirty and vandalized bathrooms are the norm. Facilities are often very unhygienic and badly maintained, and many are missing necessary supplies, which can lead to increased spread of infections. Boys and girls often have to walk long distances in the school in order to get to the bathroom. Bathrooms are also a hotspot for bullies who take advantage of the lack of supervision and use them as a location to target and intimidate vulnerable students. Because of these poor conditions in school bathrooms many students are unwilling to use them and refuse to go all day. In addition, some students refuse to consume beverages during the school day in order to avoid using the bathroom, which can expose them to the risks of dehydration, as well as bladder and bowel problems.

Currently, some schools try to combat problems like gathering and bad behavior in bathrooms by closing facilities for part of the day to maintain school safety and discipline. The partitions between bathroom stalls and the doors that lead to them are absurdly small and sometimes schools even take doors off bathroom stalls altogether to "improve security." Such measures further exacerbate the problem of students not using the bathrooms, which is inhumane and cruel considering that most school days last between six and eight hours and usually will contain at least one meal. For students to be subjected to the kind of humiliation normally associated with a high-security prison, all in the name of safety, speaks volumes about a bankruptcy of ideas when it comes to school design.

So what is the solution? Let's start with the nomenclature because this sends a strong signal about our design philosophy. We have intentionally used the word "bathrooms" juxtaposed with the word "home-like" to immediately disconnect our design from the institutional environment associated with the problems discussed above. We believe that clean, hygienic and safe bathrooms are an essential part of a positive education experience. Along with setting aside the resources to ensure proper facility maintenance, there are a number of simple design choices we can make to minimize or even completely eliminate the problems associated with badly designed school bathrooms. These are described in our Pattern for Home-Like Bathrooms (Figure 25-3).

The first step to combating bullying and gathering in bathrooms is to provide effective supervision without infringing on students' rights to privacy. There are three components to accomplishing this. First, the bathrooms must be small and distributed throughout the school with a maximum of two to five stalls at each location. Second, each bathroom should ideally be located adjacent to a fully supervised commons area, such as those included within a Small Learning Community. Third, the access door to the bathroom should be transparent, permitting passive supervision from the commons area. As with the design of the bathroom at St. Aloysius High School in Tasmania (Figure 25-2), the transparent door would open into a small hallway off of which the actual bathroom stalls would be located. Instead of having sinks in this area, as is the norm in most institutional bathrooms, the hallway would contain no activities or services. The only reason a student would be standing in this visible space would be to wait for a stall to become free. That said, there is no reason why the bathroom should be an aesthetically boring place. Each bathroom could be decorated and personalized by the students who use it. Bathrooms should be well-lit, cheerful and colorful. They are also excellent places to display student artwork. Where possible, daylight should be introduced into the bathroom hallway.

Once inside the stall, a student would find full privacy as found in residential bathrooms, with the walls of the stall extending all the way to the ceiling and the door closing completely to the floor, like all regular doors. This increased sense of privacy would eliminate the anxiety students currently face in bathrooms where a bully or someone else can easily peek into a stall and cause embarrassment. The stall would contain all the necessary elements within it, namely a toilet, sink, mirror, hand-dryer and trash bin so that the entire process of "going to the bathroom" takes place in a private, secure area which students can immediately leave once done. Each stall also contains a hook in order to keep students' personal belongings off the bathroom floor. The space within each stall is sufficient but minimal, in order to discourage students from gathering inside stalls. The floor-to-ceiling design also discourages students from communicating between stalls and passing illegal items between stalls. Where water conservation is important, we recommend that waterless urinals be placed inside the stalls of boys' bathrooms.

To alleviate concerns about sick students trapped within stalls or students locking themselves in a stall, adult supervisors should be able to open stalls from the outside using a special key. Schools may also wish to install simple manual or digital timers on stalls that would sound an alarm if they remain locked for an extended period of time. Some loss of privacy in the interest of safety may be an acceptable compromise accomplished by not extending entrance doors all the way to the floor. However, even in such cases, we recommend that the floor-to-ceiling partitions between stalls be retained.

Our children spend most of their days for many years of their lives in school buildings. They should be nurturing, caring places where students are encouraged to develop socially, emotionally and academically. But none of this would be possible unless the simple, natural routine of going to the bathroom becomes no more stressful or complicated than it is at home.

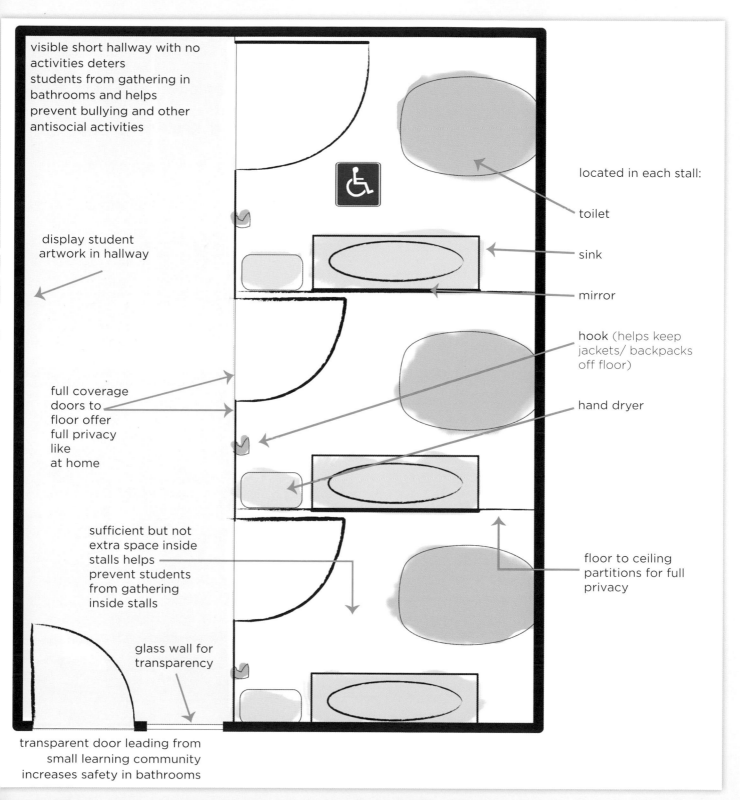

visible short hallway with no activities deters students from gathering in bathrooms and helps prevent bullying and other antisocial activities

display student artwork in hallway

full coverage doors to floor offer full privacy like at home

sufficient but not extra space inside stalls helps prevent students from gathering inside stalls

glass wall for transparency

transparent door leading from small learning community increases safety in bathrooms

located in each stall:

toilet

sink

mirror

hook (helps keep jackets/ backpacks off floor)

hand dryer

floor to ceiling partitions for full privacy

Figure 25-3.
Design Pattern #25: Home-like Bathrooms.

Design Pattern 26 — Teachers as Professionals

In 2007, McKinsey & Co. commissioned a global study of the practices of the world's most effective education systems. McKinsey concluded that the factor that made the greatest difference in student achievement was the quality, support and development of the system's teaching force, and the country that did this best was Finland.

Views and Vistas

Conference table and white board for teacher collaboration

Ability to make private phone calls

Multiple personal storage options (e.g. shelving, rolling storage, locked storage)

Wireless network available to support mobile technology

Figure 26-1.
Design Pattern #26: Teachers as Professionals.

Teaching is a profession. It requires in most jurisdictions a four-year degree at least, and many teachers have more than one degree. Teachers are required to work in teams and to participate in ongoing professional development. Yet the working environments of most teachers are nowhere near on par with those of equivalent professionals in other industries. Particularly if teachers are expected to engage in a significant change in pedagogical paradigms, it is only reasonable that they too have ergonomic, flexible working environments. See Figure 26-1.

This means that teachers need dedicated offices and storage space, preferably with the same ergonomic standards (lighting, ventilation, acoustics, views and vistas, furniture) as applied to principal learning areas. They also need space to meet in team groups, and facilities for lesson and project preparation. Teacher offices rarely provide adequate access to ICT, or the power access to support it.

Staff lounges are desirable, and in most cases fiercely protected with good reason. They are not necessarily sacred though. Depending on the nature of relationships the school seeks to foster among its communities, and the size of the school, one big staff room may not be the best

way of catering to them. Best-case scenarios are illustrated in Figures 26-2 and 26-3.

Figure 26-2 (far left).
Teachers have ample workspace and views from three-quarters of the walls at Duke School, NC.

Figure 26-3 (above).
A space dedicated to assessment and recordkeeping, shared by all teachers in this Kindergarten-level Small Learning Community (Wooranna Park Primary School, Melbourne, Australia).

Shared Learning Resources and Library

Young children are usually very good at using whatever materials are around to learn with—how often have you seen kids using sticks, trees, steps, furniture or wrapping paper for playing games or telling stories? The simplest materials are often the most useful learning tools because their use isn't prescribed or implied.

Figure 27-1.

Design Pattern #27: Shared Learning Resources and Library.

a) Multi-media displays capable of sharing real-time information; b) Traditional print resources available not only in library/media center, but throughout the campus; c) Wired and wireless digital network available to support work across campus; d) Learning breakout and peer tutoring spaces are media and information-rich.

Figure 27-2 (bottom left).

Students and teachers can easily find a variety of learning resources at Duke School throughout the day.

Learning resources are really any material that can be used for learning. In the context of school though, the term is typically applied to electronic (hardware, software, or online publications), printed (books, magazines and newspapers) or manipulative (e.g. counters, games, dress-ups, construction toys) resources.

There are two key components to effective management of learning resources. One is that the resources themselves are relevant and useful, and the other is that they are accessible. The first of these matters is not architectural, but planners should note that the best teachers will see potential for all sorts of authentic materials to enhance learning, not just rare/costly/prescriptive items. See Figure 27-1.

It's all very well to have a brilliant set of resources, but that's no use if it can't be accessed by the right students and teachers at the right time. Traditionally schools have held the bulk of their resources in central libraries, which are great for keeping stock, but not necessarily great for allowing easy, independent access. Library use tends towards scheduled class sessions in the library, which supports a 'just in case' model of curriculum delivery, rather than a 'just in time' exploration of learning opportunities.

A principal with much foresight called for his library to be housed in the school's main entrance—a space which doubled as a cafeteria and thoroughfare. "But you can't!" cried the librarian. "All the books will be stolen!" The principal replied, "I will measure the success of this library according to the number of books that go missing. I want our students to value books!"

Where students are able to access the library independently, there are still often issues with unsupervised travel around the school, and even when that is not a problem, students invariably have to ask a teacher if they can go to the library. This may not appear to be a problem, but consider briefly the hidden curriculum here: "The teacher is the gatekeeper of your learning—you are not an independent learner."

So, when every available space in a school is a classroom or a corridor, a central library is one of the more accessible ways to store learning resources—when classrooms are being used for formal instruction there is no scope for anyone (from that classroom or another) to access the resources within. Alternatively, once the traditional structure has been dismantled, the opportunities for greater accessibility can begin to be realized. See Figure 27-2.

The Future of the School Library

The following is an excerpt from the Introduction to *Rethink!* Nair, P & Gehling, A (2007). Edited by La Marca, S. School Library Association of Victoria.

Good libraries have always been places where personalized learning has taken place (also see Figure 9-7). The hidden curriculum of traditional school architecture, with its long corridors and inflexible box-like classrooms, sends messages such as, 'Learning happens under the constant supervision of one all-knowing teacher' and 'you are not responsible for your own learning.' Good libraries, on the other hand, have a variety of spaces for individuals and small groups to work together and often have places for larger group presentations as well. Of course, they are also text-rich. The message in this type of architecture is, 'Here are some of the tools for you to learn with. You are a trusted learner. Go for it!'

Most of our work is in redesigning schools so that the architecture supports a productive hidden curriculum. Surprise, surprise, the spaces we end up with often look more like today's best libraries than yesterday's best schools.

The current revolution in school learning spaces is long overdue, but it will be many years before all students are touched by a humanizing curriculum, supported by humanizing spaces. In the meantime, libraries will be the place where students can engage in their own projects, explore topics and texts at their own pace, according to their own interests, on their own whims.

But wait... we have the opportunity to do that here and now! With the Internet now a ubiquitous presence in our lives, we must bring up that old chestnut... what's the point of a library when surely the information I\we want is available to us anywhere we have a computer or mobile phone?

Let us attempt to answer this question. The internet is like a library in many respects. Some things it does better than a library: it isn't as physically restricted, it contains far, far more information than the largest library in the world; it can be accessed by far more people than that library physically can be. And, most importantly, is has democratized media delivery and creation in a way never seen before.

A library can do some things better than the Internet. A good library not only has answers to our questions, past and present and future (as the Internet can usually provide), it has a place, a physical domain in which we can become absorbed in those answers. A good library makes interacting with texts of all kinds irresistible. It's comfortable and peaceful. Particularly for children, it is rare to be in a space in which the rules and expectations are not controlled by others. The space of the classroom is controlled by the teacher. Libraries are, in a sense, the domain of librarians, but use of the space is up to the user: kids generally don't just walk in, sit down and wait to be directed or spoon-fed by the 'owner' of the space.

It has humans in it! One of the greatest things about so-called Internet 2.0 applications such as Facebook, YouTube and MySpace is their focus on sharing. It might sound a little like this: 'I love this book, I think you'd like it too!' 'I know you like making things, Jonathan, I found this magazine online that's all about making things!' 'Wow, the director of that YouTube film had some great ideas about furniture!' and 'What did you think of the latest Harry Potter movie?' Libraries, similarly, are all about sharing: connecting people with others and resources that might just feed a passion or spark an idea. Librarians—real people who know their clientele (especially in the case of a school), have some idea of the scope of resources available and can help students find and navigate their way through them—add so much beyond the sheer power of the internet.

Without a doubt, libraries will continue to evolve. The purpose and experience of libraries will change, and change again, in their physical and virtual iterations.

One key change is already well underway and this is the opportunity to link school and community via the library. This trend is beginning to catch on throughout the world and that is because there are few places in a community that lend themselves more easily to joint school/community use than the library. An excellent example of this can be found in Mawson Lakes, Adelaide (Figure 27-3) where the community library serves residents and students of all ages from pre-kindergarten through secondary school and university.

Figure 27-3.

This Library at Mawson Lakes, Adelaide, serves students of all ages from pre-kindergarten through University as well as community residents.

School Safety

In December 2012, the deadly assault by a troubled, armed loner on Sandy Hook Elementary School in Newtown, CT, where 20 children and six adults were killed, riveted the American consciousness and resulted in renewed anxiety about the safety of our children while they are in school. Across the nation, at school district meetings, town hall meetings, online forums and in the media, people have been trying to find better ways to ensure school safety. Possible ideas have included placing guards at entrances, installing hotlines to first responders and better perimeter control.

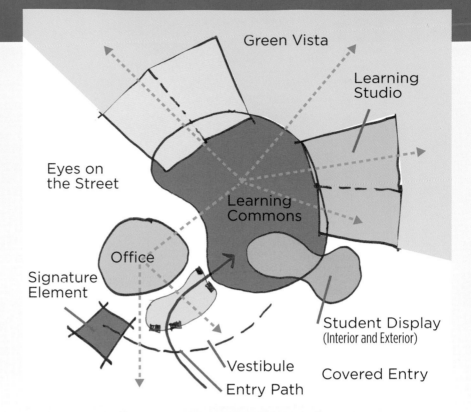

Figure 28-1.
Design Pattern #29: Overlapping Principles for Safety and Security

Bottom Left:
Step Dancing in the Community Commons, Cristo Rey High School, Minneapolis, Minnesota.

The US Department of Education Office of Safe and Drug-free Schools Guidelines lists a number of common school safety limitations, including "easy access into schools," "staff unable to spot threats in time," and "victims had inadequate escape paths." These limitations are exacerbated by the traditional, crowd-control-oriented design of most schools, which calls for double-loaded corridors lined with numerous single entrances to enclosed classrooms.

But the solution to these limitations does not lie in pushing children more deeply into an otherwise completely self-contained box. Safety can be robustly designed into the physical features and social culture of a school, even as its spaces are made more accessible to adjacent interior and exterior spaces. We should always keep our eye on maintaining and protecting the quality of learning and thriving that come from being a valued member of a nurturing community. This sense of belonging can negate or minimize feelings of resentment and alienation that can lead a troubled individual to retaliate against the impersonal, faceless system that he or she failed to navigate successfully.

Five overlapping principles should be considered when designing or retrofitting a school building for safety. Each of these principles can help slow an assailant's progress, alert school staff to quickly identify potential trouble and allow for better student escape. Unlike armed guards, these principles can also help a school welcome the local community, create a home-like environment and support multiple learning modalities.

Five Overlapping Principles of Secure Design
1. Eyes on the Street
2. Welcoming, Secure Entrance
3. Transparency
4. Learning Space Configuration
5. Safe Community Involvement

"...there must be eyes upon the street, eyes belonging to those we might call the natural proprietors of the street. The buildings on a street equipped to handle strangers and to insure the safety of both residents and strangers, must be oriented to the street. They cannot turn their backs or blank sides on it and leave it blind."

- Jane Jacobs, *The Death and Life of Great American Cities*

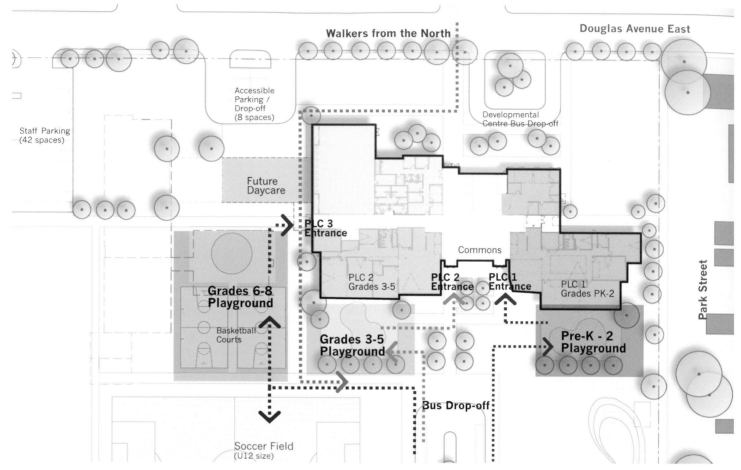

Figure 28-2 (above).

Douglas Park School in Regina, Saskatchewan is designed so that all playgrounds can be easily supervised by one playground attendant, and the school office is located with clear views of the public entrance.

Eyes on the Street

The best way for a school to be safe is for adults to be able to see everywhere and everyone. The traditional school model is hardly conducive to having control over a large space, as it seeks to separate a school community into small identical groups, positioned behind a single door with no views into the classroom beyond a window in that door. Designing interiors and exteriors with wide and long sightlines enables school staff to spot threats, including the far more likely scenario of student bullying than of an intruder with sinister motives.

Welcoming, Secure Entrance

To ensure that as many adults as possible can passively monitor the entry area, both inside and out, the school office should ideally be located immediately inside the front entrance, with large windows that face the approach and door overhang. This allows school staff to monitor the entrance, rather than be tucked away in an enclosed office behind a single door. This solution can be built into a new school, or retrofitted into an existing school by strategically replacing portions of the walls with glass.

Figure 28-3 (left).
Exterior lighting allows school staff to see from inside or outside.

Figure 28-4 (below).
At this school in Medford, Oregon, the school office is oriented towards both the front entrance and school commons.

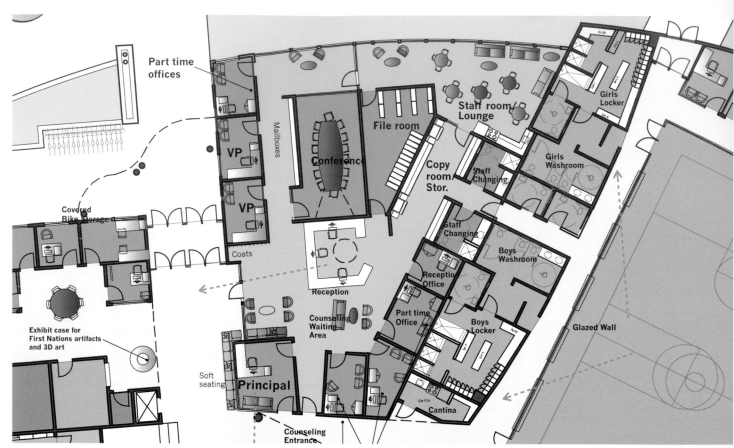

Part time offices

VP

VP

Mailboxes

Conference

Coats

File room

Copy room/ Stor.

Staff room/ Lounge

Staff Changing

Girls Locker

Girls Washroom

Staff Changing

Boys Washroom

Covered Bike Storage

Reception

Counseling Waiting Area

Reception Office

Part time Office

Boys Locker

Glazed Wall

Exhibit case for First Nations artifacts and 3D art

Soft seating

Principal

Cantina

Counseling Entrance

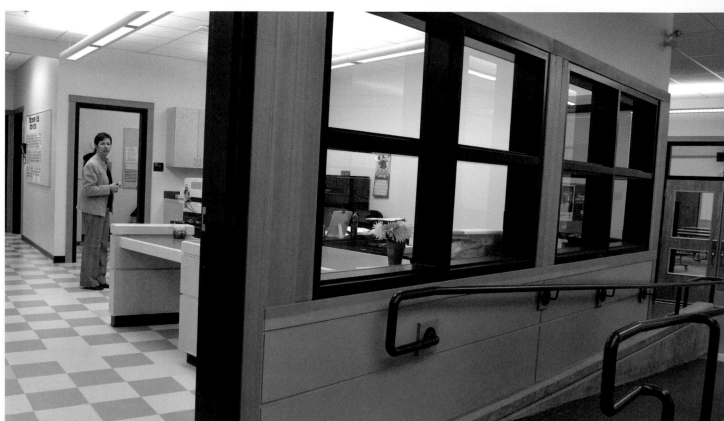

Figure 28-5 (top left).
FH Collins Secondary School in the Yukon Territory is designed to welcome visitors and orient them. The entrance is easily seen from the main street. The school office has a clear view of the front entrance, and if necessary, can electronically control the doors.

Figure 28-6 (bottom left).
This school office in an elementary school in Vancouver has interior windows that overlook the entrance and community commons.

Figure 28-7 (below).
Interior windows allow teachers to monitor students in this project space.

Transparency

The concept of transparency in schools has been criticized recently, in response to the issue of targeted assaults on schools. These criticisms focus on the idea that interior and even exterior windows should be blocked, so intruders can't see inside and identify potential victims. But blocking off windows isolates people from each other and from other spaces in the school. This could be an even more dangerous scenario in the highly unlikely event of an attack.

In addition, blocking off windows would block off natural daylight and views to the outside which are known to have a calming effect on the human brain. The net result would mean a deterioration in the quality of the daily social, emotional, behavioral and academic experience of the children, a very high price to pay for a questionable security solution.

We don't want our need to keep certain people out of the school to inadvertently sabotage our need to allow certain people into the school who offer valuable resources and skills to both students and teachers. The solution to this is transparency of school spaces, which allows people into the school to work with students, but under the constant supervision of school staff.

Learning Space Configuration

Just as traditional classroom configurations no longer well support 21st century learning, they are also not conducive to school safety. In this school, rather than a double-loaded corridor, the elementary school wing is now divided into a group of varied spaces centered around a larger commons area, shared by a community of students and teachers. Most of the learning spaces have more than one way in and out, and many studios can even open to the outside with lockable doors. Evasion from danger creates better outcomes, particularly in the case of fire.

A Learning Community model, at approximately 150 students, is small enough so that everyone knows each other. Students store their belongings in the commons area of their Learning Community, where all students and teachers can keep an eye on them. This results in less stolen student property, as students self-police the community and manage themselves as if anyone could be watching them at any given moment.

Safe Community Involvement

School campuses should offer a variety of multi-purpose spaces for those within the immediate school community including parents, teachers, and students. School facilities should also cater to the needs of their extended stakeholder community, including community residents and local businesses, for activities such as meetings, volunteer work, play, or evening events and classes. After hours access should be restricted to elements of the campus that are shared with the community such as the media center, cafeteria, gymnasium, auditorium and playgrounds.

Figure 28-8 (top left).
Multiple sliding doors open from this Learning Community onto an outdoor learning terrace.

Figure 28-9 (above).
Nooks and window-seats create a home-like atmosphere, providing safe places for students to work quietly and feel secure.

Figure 28-10 (right).
This elementary public school commons provides a safe place for community volunteers to tutor students, under the constant supervision of school staff.

Bringing It All Together

One of the big benefits of the Design Pattern Method is that it allows the planning team to develop ideas at different scales. This makes it possible to work on an individual element of a school while simultaneously keeping an eye on how those elements interact—with each other, with the whole school and with the larger community.

Figure 29-1.

Design Pattern #29a: Bringing It All Together. Preliminary Design Pattern developed at community charette for Morriss Center High School, NY.

Bottom Left:

Opening Day Ceremonies. New Middle School at Scotch Oakburn College, Tasmania with amphitheater in the foreground.

An effective forum for the use of the Pattern Language is a design charette where all the key stakeholders assemble under one roof to work directly on the school design. Facilitated by the design team, the charette should begin with a discussion of the various patterns such as those included in this book that represent best practice. In the ensuing discussions, the philosophical direction of the team will become apparent, but so too will the design intent that best suits that philosophy.

After this "benchmarking" exercise, the charette can move to design criteria that are even more specific. This portion of the charette can focus on questions of functionality—in other words, how exactly the community envisions the use of the facilities and campus.

Architects can "translate" these discussions and ideas into very rough "patterns" as in Figure 29-1. Sometimes when people see their ideas graphically represented in this way, they get a better sense of what they really need and begin to ask for changes. The best thing about simple sketches is that members from the participating client community can themselves mark them up.

More developed sketches can follow to the point where consensus can be built around specific patterns for the whole campus, as well as its various elements. These rough sketches, such as in Figure 29-3, can then be developed into more refined finished patterns by the architects as in Figure 29-4. It is the early sketches that can become the blueprint against which the actual design of the school can be measured. This system allows the kind of continuity between envisioning and design that is often lost in the process of creating a school.

The three diagrams included in Figures 29-1, 29-3 and 29-4 (Design Patterns #29a, #29b and #29c) show how the Pattern Language Method helped create a design pattern that accurately reflects the community's aspirations.

The first two diagrams show the actual sketches as they developed with direct community participation and markups during the charette, and the third diagram is the design pattern for the whole school facility. This pattern informs the design as it proceeds to the next level of development.

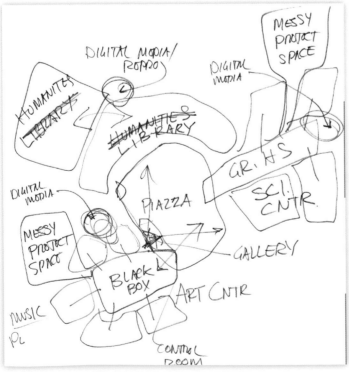

Figure 29-2 (above).
Welcoming main entrance Piazza at Canning Vale Community College in Western Australia.

Figure 29-3 (top left).
Design Pattern #29b: Bringing It All Together. Further development of Design Pattern at the charette for Morriss Center High School.

Figure 29-4 (right).
Design Pattern #29c: Bringing It All Together. Architect's sketch based upon the charette for Morriss Center High School.

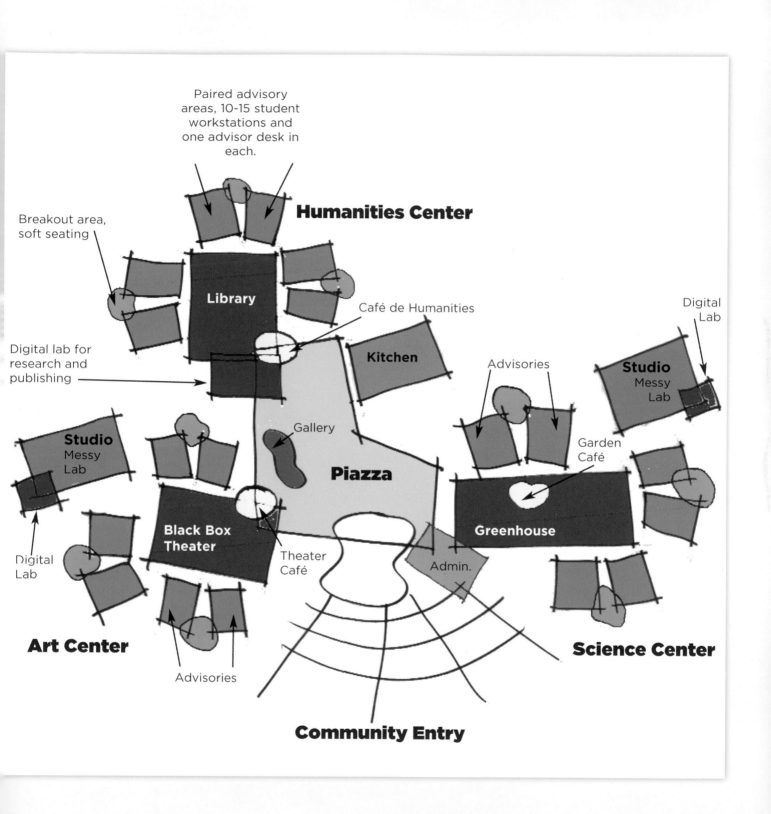

Paired advisory areas, 10-15 student workstations and one advisor desk in each.

Breakout area, soft seating

Humanities Center

Library

Digital lab for research and publishing

Café de Humanities

Kitchen

Digital Lab

Studio
Messy Lab

Advisories

Studio
Messy Lab

Gallery

Garden Café

Piazza

Digital Lab

Black Box Theater

Theater Café

Admin.

Greenhouse

Art Center

Advisories

Science Center

Community Entry

Throughout this book, we have described leading practices in education and architecture, stressing how the two must work in tandem in order to create effective schools. We have illustrated these leading practices using many specific examples and case studies.

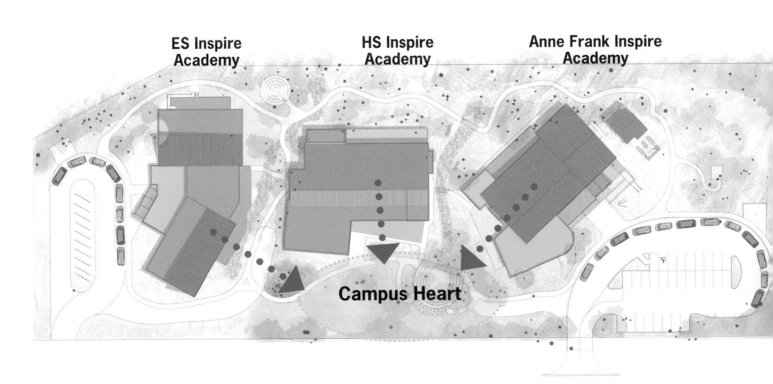

ES Inspire Academy

HS Inspire Academy

Anne Frank Inspire Academy

Campus Heart

Figure 30-1.
This site plan shows how the three schools on the campus share a campus heart with an amphitheater at its core. Each school also has generous views toward the campus heart.

Right:
For it to work and be the runaway success it became, the iPAD could not take its cues from the hardware that was already available.

However, in our estimation, there is no one single school anywhere in the world (at least none that we have ever seen) that would qualify as a 10:10. By 10:10 we mean a school that is a "10" on the educational best practices scale, complemented by a school facility that would also qualify as a "10" in that it represents the best architectural design to complement the educational practice. A 10:10 must be created from the ground up—in other words, you cannot start with a "10" educational model and design a "10" physical design around it, because a "10" educational model would be impossible without the corresponding space in which it could be conducted. By the same token, you cannot simply design a "10" school facility because that designation would be meaningless in the absence of an educational model that demanded such a design. That would explain why there are few educators clamoring for a truly innovative school design.

All this comes back to the iPAD analogy. For it to work and be the runaway success it became, the iPAD could not take its cues from the hardware that was already available. On the other hand, why create a new form factor when all the existing software was perfectly suited to the existing hardware? Wouldn't the best chance of success be to refine the existing hardware so that it could better run the existing software? Yes, but that would not be an iPAD, which is a whole new "system" that <u>meets needs people did not even know they had</u>.

Beyond that, the iPAD is also enabling people to do things they used to do before on a PC or a laptop a lot faster and more effectively. That means the new "system" of computing represented by the iPAD and the apps that run on it did not require a radical departure in all the computing that people used to do. The new form factor still allowed people to browse websites, send and receive emails, watch videos, create documents and connect on social networking sites, but it meant that these things could now be done better and faster and in situations where a laptop or a netbook would have been impractical or cumbersome.

If the iPAD had stopped there and simply made traditional computing tasks easier or more accessible, it would have been a hit, but of course we know it went much farther. The new form factor meant a whole new world of possibilities—and we now have tens of thousands of apps to prove it. The iPAD thus redefined the computing landscape entirely but what brought about this change? The form factor or the software (apps)? The answer is both. The iPAD needed both its form factor with its own natural "language" of swipes, pinches and clicks and a new way to access software (apps) to be developed together and work harmoniously for its success.

This is exactly true of schools but perhaps the urgency of an iPAD version of the school building is even more overdue. Like the iPAD, this new version of school must be started as a whole new "system." Naturally, it will be difficult to introduce a brand new system within the cultural context of existing educational institutions. These institutions are already operating within a system, most of the pieces of which they are quite comfortable with—even when they complain about less-than-satisfactory student outcomes. Change is difficult, because the challenge encompasses not just a new environment for learning (21st century school buildings) but also leadership, curriculum, pedagogy, scheduling, staffing, professional development, assessment, community involvement, political support and parent education.

One would be wrong to conclude that the rest of this book is not valuable just because it is not directed exclusively to those interested in completely changing the educational paradigm. Even as iPAD sales are through the roof, so also laptop and netbooks are selling briskly. For the time being at least, there is room for both paradigms to co-exist. The practical ideas contained in this book can make good schools much better and more effective at delivering a 21st century education even if they are not looking for radical transformations. In fact, the primary audience for this book is all the schools that want to do better but realize that paradigm-shifting transformation may be a few years away.

A 10:10 Case Study

We had said at the beginning of this chapter that we have never seen a 10:10 school, but we truly believe that is about to change. This chapter is about one case study which represents a new model built from the ground up, not unlike the iPAD, that will be a true 10:10 school. It has the potential not only to change the way we look at school buildings but at the whole enterprise we call education. We believe this case study is important to share because it provides a peek at what we're certain is the future of education itself. We fully expect several hundred schools to be developed along these lines within the next few years and, once the model attains a certain critical mass, it can garner enough momentum to change the United States' education system entirely. Given the global world in which we live, that also means it's a model that many other countries will surely adopt as well.

Inspire Academies, San Antonio, Texas

Appropriately named, Inspire Academies is a whole new kind of charter school whose vision is best described by founding Superintendent Bruce Rockstroh. In his own words, "*I am more committed than ever to build and design the exemplary 21st century school that will become a model for learning around the world.*

Paul Goldberger recently affirmed that 'the place where people meet to seek the highest is holy ground' and the Anne Frank Inspire Academy will become that place: a 'Learning Building' and community that will celebrate human aspiration and greatness.

Every student we touch will be inspired to become an expert learner, a person of character and principle, a leader focused on their gifts and dedicated to finding their passion, and taught to seek a life of mission and service for the greater good. These are the components of greatness in our time and to which we will dedicate ourselves and our vision. It is a sacred task, carving out this unique, special place. I have no doubt that all who touch this school—students, parents, teachers, the community—will have their lives changed."

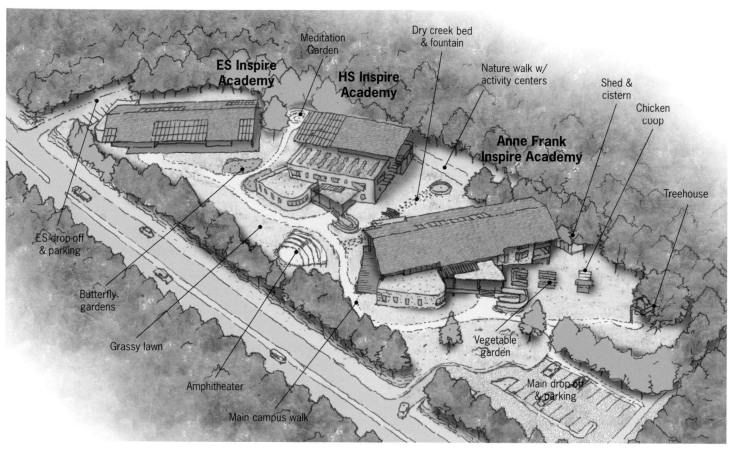

Meditation Garden

Dry creek bed & fountain

ES Inspire Academy

HS Inspire Academy

Nature walk w/ activity centers

Shed & cistern

Chicken coop

Anne Frank Inspire Academy

Treehouse

ES drop-off & parking

Butterfly gardens

Grassy lawn

Amphitheater

Main campus walk

Vegetable garden

Main drop-off & parking

Figure 30-2.

Bird's eye view of the conceptual design shows the Anne Frank Inspire Academy co-located with two other semi-autonomous schools on a small 4.7 acre site. Notice how the site is fully utilized with a variety of outdoor learning opportunities.

The Anne Frank Inspire Academy is a middle school, the first of three semi-autonomous Inspire Academies that will be located at the charter district's flagship 4.7 acre site in San Antonio. The middle school is the first phase of the overall project and is slated to open in 2013. The two other academies, an elementary school and a high school, will open in 2014. There are four notable facts about this first group of Inspire Academies.

1. None of them will enroll more than 150 students. Current plans are to start with three schools and then scale up the program to create at least 100 schools.

2. Together, the first three schools will be developed for a budget that is about 50% of what it would cost public school systems in Texas to build a facility for a comparable population.

3. The first school had to be planned, designed and constructed in about 24 months—the site had not even been purchased by the time the project kicked off and numerous government approvals would be needed before the school could be built and opened. This would have seemed like an impossible schedule when the project started, but as of this writing the school is set to open in the fall of 2014.

4. Students at Inspire Academies will have access to an education and learning facilities that will be comparable to the best private schools anywhere in the world.

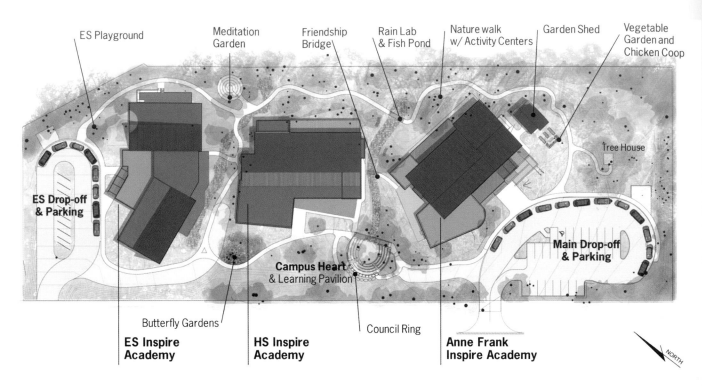

ES Playground · Meditation Garden · Friendship Bridge · Rain Lab & Fish Pond · Nature walk w/ Activity Centers · Garden Shed · Vegetable Garden and Chicken Coop

Tree House

ES Drop-off & Parking

Campus Heart & Learning Pavilion

Main Drop-off & Parking

Butterfly Gardens

Council Ring

ES Inspire Academy · **HS Inspire Academy** · **Anne Frank Inspire Academy**

NORTH

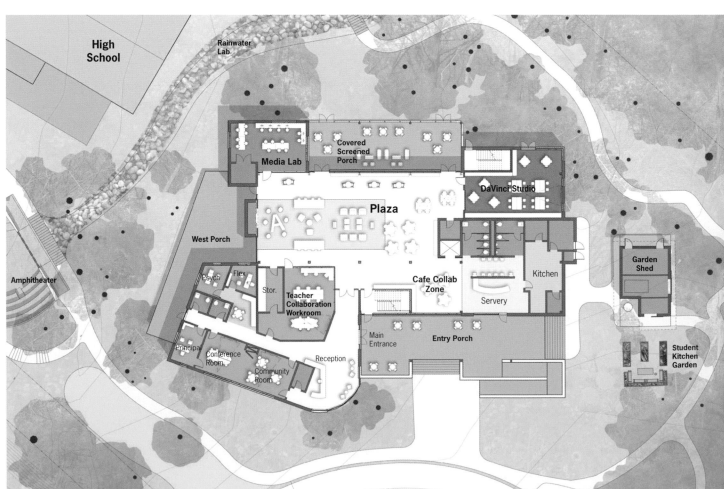

High School

Rainwater Lab

Media Lab

Covered Screened Porch

DaVinci Studio

Plaza

West Porch

Psych · Flex

Stor.

Teacher Collaboration Workroom

Cafe Collab Zone

Kitchen

Servery

Amphitheater

Principal · Conference Room

Main Entrance

Entry Porch

Reception

Community Room

Garden Shed

Student Kitchen Garden

About the Process

Very early in the planning process, Superintendent Rockstroh and his team realized that the physical campus for the first group of Inspire Academies would be critical to the success of the new educational model they were looking to plan and implement. At the same time, they also realized that it would be critical to create a new model that was cost effective—perhaps even be done for half of what traditional public schools cost. Otherwise, their schools, no matter how successful, would be dismissed as being too expensive and the model would have difficulties replicating and scaling up.

With these ideas in mind, the team went about the task of finding a group of architects and educators with a track record for innovation. The key from day one was to keep the discussion focused on educational practice and what learning might look like at the school. With both educators and architects in the mix, it was possible to test architectural ideas for their educational efficacy and educational ideas for their architectural ramifications. One of the first things we discussed was the proposed signature of the school—Superintendent Rockstroh proposed that the first middle school be named The Anne Frank Inspire Academy. In his mind, Anne Frank, herself a middle school student, had the goodness, courage and strength of character to serve as a superb role model for the students attending the school.

Figure 30-3.
The final Master plan shows the correct placement of the buildings and the various site improvements. The trails running through the site allow students to explore the meditation garden, fish pond, rainwater lab, and treehouse while experiencing the natural landscape of the site.

Figure 30-4.
This ground floor plan shows how the whole school is oriented around a central Plaza with a variety of zones and bordered by a Da Vinci Studio and several learning decks.

The Site Walk

This was one of the first exercises of the team and it was led by the architects. It resulted in several valuable observations. Here are just a few of the design ideas that emerged from the site walk.

1. We noticed that even though the site was elevated from a local highway, traffic noise at the front of the site could be a problem. So we discussed ways in which this problem could be alleviated—settling for earth berms and an amphitheater that would shield the buildings from the noise.

2. We observed many significant trees and started to formulate a plan for the ones we would want to preserve. We also discussed the idea of a "treehouse" as a playful element on the site but one that would be significant, because Anne Frank herself wrote lovingly about an old chestnut tree outside her window.

3. We noticed an old barn on the site and a capped well and made notes to see if these could somehow be used as part of the design.

4. We observed the various naturally growing plants and wild flowers and decided to incorporate as many of these species as possible in the landscaping plan. We married this to an idea for a nature trail featuring the local species which could be integrated into the science curriculum.

5. We saw that a neighbor had goats on his property and decided to speak to him about allowing the goats to graze on our property as well so that students could enjoy their presence at the school.

6. We noticed two large, leased billboards on the property and decided we would want them removed before the start of construction.

7. We made notes regarding the site elevations (which sections were higher with better vistas and which ones

were lower and closer to street level) and talked about potential places where traffic would enter and leave the site.

8. It was obvious to us that the scale of the site would allow three 150-student schools to be comfortably co-located there but that there would not be room for large playfields. It led to a discussion about using community facilities for extracurricular activities.

9. We then visited a local park which has numerous play facilities, with ball fields and a large indoor athletic complex housing a swimming pool that got very little use during the day. It would be much cheaper to make a "use agreement" with this organization than to duplicate these expensive facilities on the school site (which was much too small for these facilities anyway). A decision was made to limit the site to fitness activities and use the community facilities for larger athletic programs and sporting events.

Design Charette

Inspired by the site walk, we returned to the charter school offices for a design charette where the design team began to sketch the possibilities for putting three schools on the site. Using some rule of thumb estimates for how many square feet per student we would need while keeping one eye on the available budget, we quickly calculated how big each school building might be and what the footprint of each school would be if we limited them to two stories.

Based on what we had learned from our site walk, we started a rough arrangement of buildings on site, figuring out things like site entry, a suitable area for parking, and the relationship between the three schools on campus. We also talked about how much of the site we could afford to build in phase one by the time the middle school opened.

The most important discussion about the way in which the school would be designed and operated happened during this first design charette. It was at this session that we proposed flipping the traditional schooling model on its head. A vast majority of schools (even those that aspire to be 21st century schools) start with the idea that all lessons and by extension all learning begins in a classroom or a learning studio. While students are afforded the opportunity to take their learning to other spaces in the schools, these other places are always seen as being subordinate to the classroom whose primacy as the center of the learning experience is never questioned. That means, learning always starts and ends in a classroom although students can "break out" into other spaces and explore other learning modes but only insofar as these experiences are designed to enhance the classroom learning.

For Inspire Academies we asked the group why we should allow a space (the classroom) to dictate how children learned. What if we looked at learning as a series of experiences which would vary depending on what was being learned and then allowed teachers and students to select spaces in the school that matched the needs of the learning activity at hand? What would a school look like if it dropped the assumption that all learning started and ended with a classroom? As the discussion evolved, we realized that a good way to set up the physical school would be around a "heart" which would be far more multi-faceted than a typical classroom. After going through a number of terms to describe this place, we settled on a familiar Texan notion of "The Plaza." The Plaza would be a place that students first encountered as they walked into the school and it would be a richly designed environment where a wide variety of learning experiences could happen simultaneously. We likened the design of the Plaza to a well-designed hotel lobby which has a lot of different activities all happening at the same time and yet there is a healthy buzz and energy in the space that is infectious and exciting. Where would students rather learn, in a hotel lobby Starbucks kind of place or in a box squeezed into a seat with 25 other students listening to a teacher? We thought the answer to that was obvious.

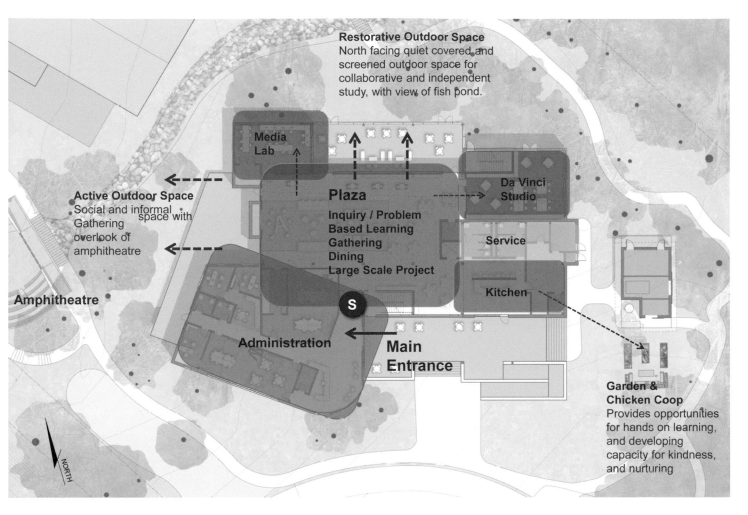

Restorative Outdoor Space
North facing quiet covered and screened outdoor space for collaborative and independent study, with view of fish pond.

Media Lab

Plaza
Inquiry / Problem Based Learning Gathering Dining Large Scale Project

Da Vinci Studio

Service

Kitchen

Active Outdoor Space
Social and informal Gathering space with overlook of amphitheatre

Amphitheatre

Administration

S

Main Entrance

Garden & Chicken Coop
Provides opportunities for hands on learning, and developing capacity for kindness, and nurturing

NORTH

Figure 30-5.

This diagram shows how the ground floor is zoned with the Plaza as the central heart surrounded by various related activities. Notice also how strongly the learning spaces are connected to project decks and outdoor learning areas.

From there, the rest of the design flowed easily. We asked ourselves what other experiences would students and teachers need that could not be properly delivered in the Plaza. This led us to create special places like a media lab, a DaVinci Studio, a lecture theater, a small group room, a seminar room, a place for dance and performance, a café and even an intimate "nest" for small group work. But our design palette extended beyond the four walls of the school building itself, and we started to draw covered and uncovered project decks with strong indoor-outdoor connections. But we did not stop there. We continued to talk about the various opportunities for outdoor learning, integrating this thinking with green (sustainable) design. This led to a series of exciting ideas for outdoor learning including the treehouse we had first discussed during our sitewalk.

As you read through this chapter and look at the design that emerged as a result of our process, you will immediately see how different it is from a traditional school design process. Those invariably begin with a group of bureaucrats telling architects precisely what can and cannot be built. Even before a project has started, it is already designed in bureaucratese. You are told how many classrooms to include, how big those classrooms need to be and exactly what they should contain, and you are given a detailed set of

Figure 30-6.

The welcoming exterior of the Anne Frank Inspire Academy features local materials like limestone and cedar timber. The lower administration area (bottom left) overlooks the entry to provide passive supervision. Students enter the building via large glass doors that lead to the community café and the rest of the learning spaces.

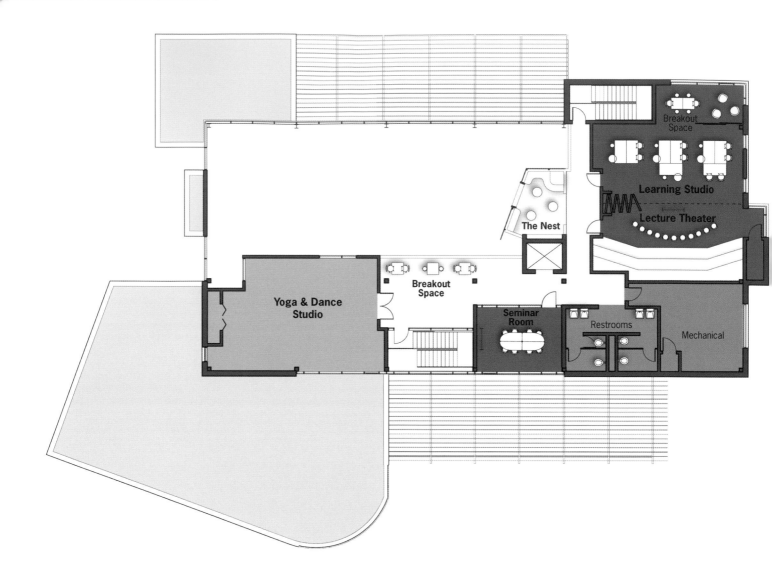

Figure 30-7.
The second floor overlooks the Plaza and contains a seminar room and lecture theater that can also be used for distance learning. This 150-student school has no traditional classrooms or hallways.

instructions for the design of every other space in the school. By the time you are done, you have masterfully duplicated yesterday's school. The future of education is almost never a part of the discussion and even if it were, the rules would hardly allow any deviation from what is set forth in the school building standards of most school districts.

This chapter shows it does not have to be that way. If you can build a world class school for half the money in half the time that it takes to create yesterday's school,

why wouldn't you want to try that? We're not suggesting that all schools should look like our design for Inspire Academies. But who knows what you will come up with in your own communities if you allowed your vision and your team's creativity drive the process as opposed to a set of stultified and obsolete rules?

It is a useful exercise to "test" our education and design solutions against the following education strategies and design principles.

Anne Frank Inspire Academy—Design Principles

1. **Welcoming:** Every aspect of the arrival experience to the site and to the three Academies has been designed from the ground up to be "welcoming." The small size of each school guarantees that no student will become anonymous. The small school size also helps create a safe and nurturing place. The variety of learning opportunities means that all students will feel included and not only those who may be "smart" under a more limited traditional definition.

2. **Versatile:** The Anne Frank Inspire Academy offers a far greater variety of learning experiences than a traditional classroom-based school. The Plaza which is the heart of the school building is an incredibly versatile environment—the epitome of a 10:10 school.

3. **Support Varying and Specific Learning Activities:** The Plaza is designed to accommodate a variety of learning activities, and it is designed to look and feel different throughout the school year depending on the learning activities going on at any given time. The Plaza is complemented by many spaces that are tailored to accommodate specific learning activities, like the dance and performance studio, the "Lecture Theater/Kiva" for lectures and presentations, small group rooms, the DaVinci Studio, the "Nest" and the Media Studio.

4. **Send Positive Messages:** From the small school size which guarantees that all students will have multiple adult role models to the caring manner in which the school caters to the varied talents, interests and passions of individual students, the design of the school sends positive messages about how much each student is cared for. In turn, this will encourage good citizenship and positive behaviors. Small schools also exert positive peer pressure which will be another assurance that students at the school will be far more likely to exhibit positive behaviors than traditional public middle schools.

Anne Frank Inspire Academy—Educational Strategies

1. **Student Success:** The "flipped" model of learning means that students will no longer feel like they are interchangeable parts in a learning factory. Direct Instruction will not disappear under the Inspire Academy model, but it will not be the single most dominant way to deliver instruction. Instead, students will each be able to connect with modes of learning that they are most comfortable with. The curriculum will be designed and delivered so that students assume more responsibility for their own learning. Learning itself will be defined as encompassing more than the mastery of content. Social and emotional development will be just as important as academic achievement, and teachers will serve as advisors and coaches.

2. **Teaching Teams:** At Inspire Academies, teachers are not isolated in classrooms. They will work collaboratively in an office with their colleagues as part of a small and manageable professional learning community. The curriculum will also be designed to take advantage of the opportunities that will be afforded for teachers to work in collaborative teams. That means students will be doing more interdisciplinary work and more real world projects that would have been difficult to do had the school been designed as a traditional classroom-centered facility.

3. **Nurturing Community:** The most important aspect of Inspire Academies from the perspective of creating a nurturing community is the size of the school. The maximum enrollment at each Academy will not exceed 150 students. This number complies with the "rule of 150" which represents an individual's "social channel capacity." According to British anthropologist Robin Dunbar, "the figure of 150 seems to represent the maximum number of individuals with whom we can have a genuinely social relationship." At 150 students, each Inspire Academy will provide an assurance that all the students in school will know each other on a

Figure 30-8.

This view within the Plaza looks toward the East wall. A variety of seating supports a variety of activities, from independent study to small group collaboration to student presentations. Glass garage doors connect the Plaza to other learning spaces such as the DaVinci studio. The "Nest" space on the second floor overlooks the Plaza, creating a visual connection to learning activities while providing a quieter space to work.

personal level and that all the teachers in the school will also know each student personally. By dismantling the veil of anonymity that is common in large schools, students are far more likely to respond to positive peer pressure and refrain from anti-social behaviors. Just as important, small schools are easier places to operate as a caring organization since individual students don't fall between the cracks. The design of the learning environment which is geared toward recognizing individual talents and interests and providing teachers with an opportunity to support students with personalized just-in-time assistance also contributes to the creation of a nurturing community.

4. **Integrated Technology:** A variety of technologies will be readily available throughout each Academy. Spaces are specifically designed for technology-based learning that run the gamut from mobile computing devices like smart phones, tablets, netbooks and laptops to high end computers in the media lab and DaVinci Studio where large screens and more powerful processing power are needed. Smart boards are strategically located so that they can be used by both teachers and students, and suites are designed with audio and video capability for distance learning and student presentations.

5. **Scheduling Choices:** The disconnect between learning goals and education delivery is clearly evidenced by the manner in which the typical school day is scheduled. Breaking up the school day into 45-minute segments is an efficient way to deliver the curriculum and "cover" the material. But it is not effective if real learning, measured by true student engagement and deep understanding, are important. Typical school scheduling also militates against collaboration between teachers and opportunities for interdisciplinary and project-based learning. So what does scheduling have to do with school design? The design for Anne Frank Inspire Academy which will operate without fixed 45-minute periods and school bells demonstrates how the creation of physical "learning communities" can provide a wide range of scheduling choices not typically available to students and teachers in traditional school buildings.

6. **Sustainable, Connected Global Network:** Inspire Academies have strong environmental connections and will encourage teachers and students to take learning outdoors as much as possible. Here are just some of the environmental features that will be available—a butterfly garden, a chicken coop, a koi pond, a dry creek bed, a treehouse, a nature trail featuring local vegetation, a meditation garden, a vegetable garden, an amphitheater and a labyrinth. Inspire Academy schools will be designed so that they can serve not only the school population but also provide facilities and services that can be used by the community. In turn, students at the school will also be accessing community resources such as the athletic facilities available at the local public park and YMCA. Field trips and internships to connect students with community resources and businesses and having community leaders become an active part of the school community as volunteers and expert teachers are also integral to the Inspire model. Inspire schools will be set up so that students and teachers will connect with information, resources and people from all around the world. Online learning will supplement the school curriculum and the school will also actively encourage inter-school activities and projects as well as national and international travel and student exchange programs.

Is the Anne Frank Inspire Academy a 10:10 School?

The first Inspire Academy that has been designed as of this writing has been created from the ground up as a 10:10 school. The Plaza is as multi-faceted a learning environment as can be found in any school around the world. Even the specialty studios like the DaVinci Studio and the Media Studio are designed to be used for a variety of purposes and activities. The generous covered outdoor decks are also extremely versatile and can be used for a number of different learning activities. If the best test of a 10:10 school is that the architect cannot predict how exactly it will be used or what specific activities the spaces will be supporting on a day-to-day basis, then indeed The Anne Frank Inspire Academy is a consummate 10:10 school.

Transferable Lessons from the Inspire Academies Case Study

It may seem premature to celebrate the "success" of a school that has not yet been built, but as architects who have worked on hundreds of schools for over 25 years, we can recognize a winner when we see one. It is also important to point out that there is no one element about the planning, design and implementation of Inspire Academies that has not already been tried successfully before. World renowned educator Professor Stephen Heppell likes to refer to these elements as the "ingredients." In Professor Heppell's view, creating a successful innovative school can be likened to creating a successful recipe. While no two schools may use the exact same ingredients or recipe for success, they can each be successful if they are building their model using tried and tested "ingredients" (methods). So let us look at the "ingredients" that are in play with Inspire Academies. It is a familiar list, and every successful school will have some version of it.

1. Hire Visionary Leader who is focused Laser-Like on Educational Value

2. Garner Community Support

3. Sign up Sponsors and Benefactors

4. Decide to Build Small—No More than 150 Students (if school is larger, then break up into sub-schools or Learning Communities of no more than 150 students)

5. Pick an Internationally Recognized Signature for the School

6. Sync Facilities and Curriculum Discussion

7. Recognize the Transformational Potential of Technology

8. Obtain Suitable (but not excessively large) Site near Community Facilities and Amenities

9. Establish a Reasonable Budget—Need not Match National Standards

10. Assemble a World-Renowned Team of Professionals

11. Give Professionals Creative Freedom

12. Get (and Keep) Everyone Involved

13. Develop Design Reflecting Local Ethos

14. Take Advantage of Available Community Resources

15. Commit to Hiring Good Teachers

16. Commit to Professional Development

17. Hire Strong Marketing Team to Get the Word Out

18. Have Plans Ready to Go to Replicate and Scale Up Your Successful Model

The above list shows why education reform is difficult, but if one small charter district in Texas can pull it off, we have to believe others can as well.

Figure 30-9.

The design features a "Nest" on the second floor. This is a partially enclosed space for small student gatherings and independent study. It overlooks the Plaza and has panoramic views to the outdoors.

Anne Frank Inspire Academy: Master Planner and Design Architect - Fielding Nair International. Executive Architect: RVK Architects. Construction Manager: Turner Construction. Client: Inspire Academies, San Antonio, TX, Superintendent — Bruce Rockstroh.

Figure 30-10.
In addition to student dining, the Café is a social and collaborative space for students, visitors, and mentors. Located near the main entrance, visitors to the school have a sense of student activity upon arrival. The Café is used all day as a place to get food and beverages and for group meetings.

Figure 30-11.
This tree house was developed by America's foremost tree house designer and author Pete Nelson. The tree house was built using cedar and indigenous materials. It features an integrated stair, a hand crafted wood slide and glass skylights that punch through the cedar shingle roof. The Inspire Schools treehouse is the first of its kind in the United States and is a distinctive signature element of the Inspire Academies' flagship campus.

Illustrations on the following pages by Kristie Anderson:

Figure 30-12.
Idea sketch for the "friendship Bridge" between the Middle and High School buildings that will span a dry creek bed that leads to a koi pond.

Figure 30-13.
This site features a labyrinth that also doubles as a meditation garden.

Figure 30-14.
This is an early rendering of the shared amphitheater which will be used for school-wide gatherings and also for student presentations and community events.

Figure 30-15.
A vegetable garden is a key site feature. Work in the garden will be integrated into the curriculum and food grown by the students will be prepared in the school kitchen.

Conclusion

The 29 patterns we have showcased here provide compelling evidence that there are, indeed, certain healthy ways in which we can approach the design of school facilities.

What we have tried to do is marry theory with practice so that every idea we have discussed can be seen in a real-world context. We have also tried to "dejargonize" this book and write it so that it requires no special expertise to read or understand.

Our focus is the learning environment, but only insofar as it is the best physical manifestation of good educational practice. We understand that in the world of education, change can be a very painful process, but we also understand that it is more palatable and feasible when that change is tied to something tangible like a new or renovated school building. That is why we see our job not only as school architects, but also as change agents.

Sometimes, it is just a matter of linking what we do in a particular location to progressive policies that have already been adopted at a different level of the educational establishment. For example, as we were contemplating the future of the replacement school for Reece High School that had been destroyed by fire, we were fortunate that we could link the community's aspirations with the state's own adopted educational model.

Tasmania's thoughtful "Essential Learnings Framework" (Figure 1) coincided with what the school community

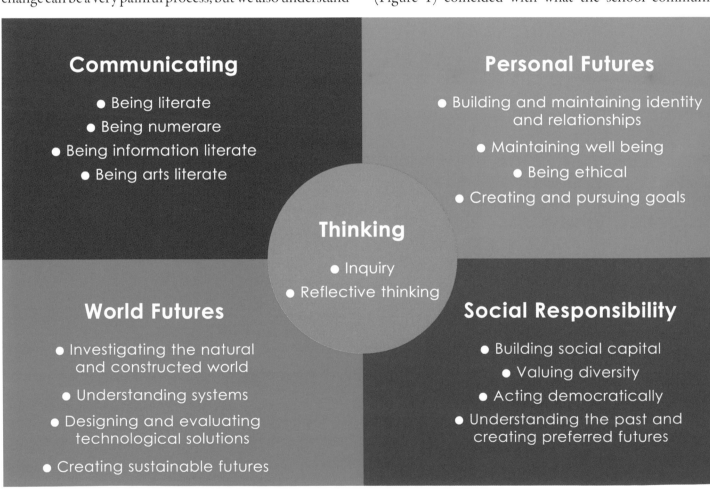

Figure 1.
"Essential Learnings Framework." (Courtesy of Tasmania Department of Education, Tasmania, Australia.)

themselves realized—that the future of education will look very different than it did in the past; that students need to learn how to think creatively, communicate well, and integrate personal goals with social responsibility in a global context.

Once we had settled on the learning goals, we were more easily able to see both the facility planning and the design of the buildings and campus as natural extensions of those goals.

The advantage of *The Language of School Design* illustrated here through the use of design patterns is that it can be done at varying levels of detail and entail as much or as little detail as may be necessary to illuminate both educational and architectural objectives. For example,

at the Goa International School, a complex set of requirements needed to be met. The client community needed a Small Learning Community-based model, which still recognized the school's signature waterfront location and its environmental science focus. The site plan, which evolved from a series of rough patterns developed during the planning workshop, reflects the seamless transition from idea to concept facilitated by the use of the Pattern Language Method. See Figure 2.

The Language of School Design, as it is presented in this book, and as it is further developed and refined over the next few years, will allow the translation of good educational ideas into built form in a manner that is much more transparent and intuitive than has ever been possible before.

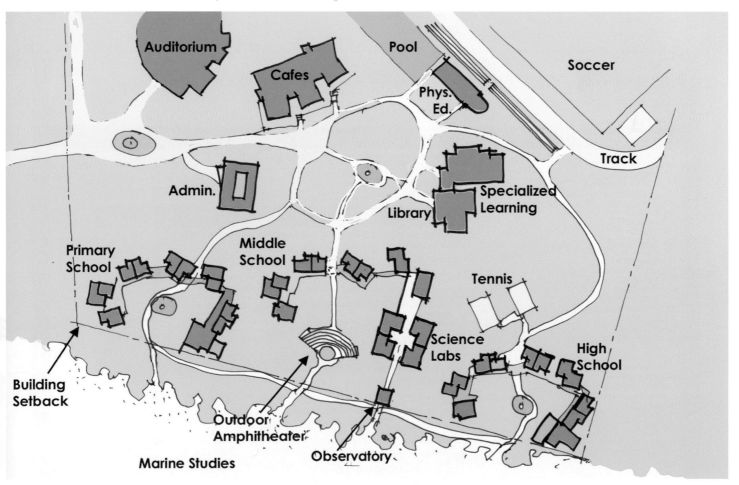

Figure 2.
Site plan for Goa International School represents the refinement of various rough design patterns.
©Fielding Nair International.

A New, Quality Measure for School Facilities
Educational Facilities Effectiveness Instrument™ (EFEI)

When we first published *The Language of School Design* in 2005, the excellent response we received was followed shortly thereafter with the occasional lament, 'But now how do I translate these patterns to my educational setting?'

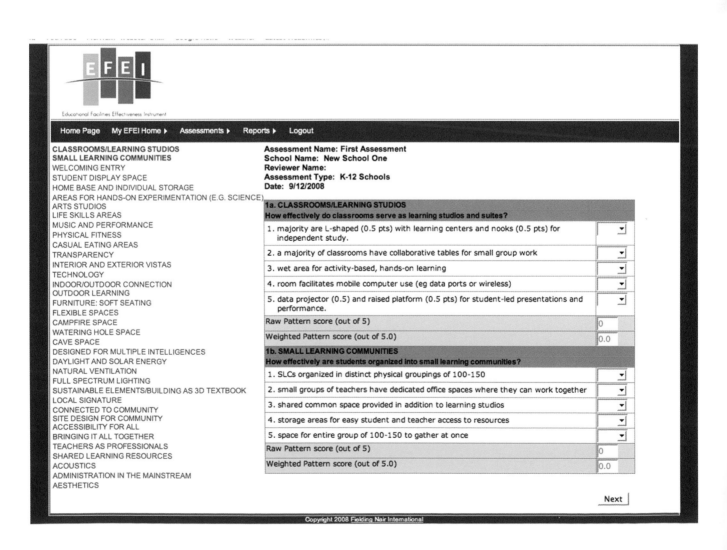

Educational Facilities Effectiveness Instrument

Design
(lighting, acoustics
furniture, ventilation,
outdoor connections,
etc.)

Utilization
(how the school can be
best utilized to support
teaching / learning)

Figure 1.
The translation of Design Pattern
Language so that it can be used to
assess existing schools, and improve
the design quality of new projects.

Figure 2 (bottom left).
An online customized template
allows users to assess and score a
design or building project utilizing
about 200 detailed checklist items.

We took up the challenge of designing an assessment tool that gave a quantitative and qualitative measure of how well an educational facility was designed according to the 25 foundation Patterns in *The Language of School Design*, and named it the *Educational Facilities Effectiveness Instrument (EFEI)*.

EFEI is unique in that it measures the most important elements of a school's design relative to its ability to support education. In the past, these elements such as a welcoming entry and strong indoor-outdoor connections had been considered un-measurable and, therefore, marginalized in the design of school facilities. EFEI allows such elements to take their rightful place as the key measures of a design's success because they are the ones most influential in any school's bottom line—its effectiveness as a place for teaching and learning.

EFEI consists of an itemized list of the pattern features in *The Language of School Design*. Each item is able to be customized or to meet the needs of each community's setting, and can be weighted according to its perceived importance in the community. Standard templates are available for the majority of formal educational settings:

early childhood, primary, middle, secondary and tertiary.

Each new client starts with customizing one of several pre-designed templates. Each template contains nearly 200 checklist items under 35 separate Design Categories. Templates can be customized by adding or deleting patterns, as well as individual features.

Performance according to each of the Patterns' features can be aggregated and the final 'score' can be used for judging the physical merits of existing or planned schools, independently or against one another. This makes EFEI useful for all types of educational building developments, at varying stages of construction. Evaluation of existing buildings can help to effectively prioritize funding arrangements, and evaluation of architectural drawings for new buildings and renovations can steer development in a learning-centered manner from the first day of design work. EFEI is also unique in that assessors can tap into a best-practice image library with hundreds of images.

EFEI provides a reliable and consistent measure of quality and is easy to understand. The criteria are based on environmental qualities of learning and living spaces that

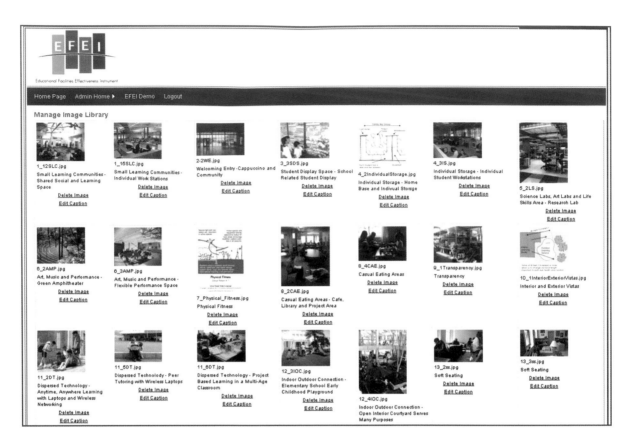

Figure 3.

The EFEI online assessment tool is supplemented by on-site and best-practice photos.

have been well researched and documented over many decades and not on current fads. At the same time EFEI can be finely tuned to the needs of each individual school and, yet, results can be compared across a region, a state, the country and even the world.

Perhaps the greatest advantage of EFEI is that it allows a school community to closely monitor the efficacy of solutions throughout the process of visioning, planning, designing, constructing, occupying, maintaining and refurbishing a school building and campus. In this way, it enables a school community to make small, but meaningful changes throughout the process which is a better guarantee of quality than a summative tool which only allows the school community to realize after the fact if a design was a success or a failure. It also allows the school stakeholder

community to "test" and "score" many different solutions on paper at a holistic campus-wide level as well as at an individual building component level very early in the planning and design stages. This kind of early testing means that costly mistakes in the later stages of a project that have a much bigger negative impact on budgets and schedules can be avoided. Used properly, EFEI can result in significant cost savings.

EFEI has already been used to evaluate over a billion dollars' worth of school facilities projects across five continents. Licenses are typically purchased by independent and government K-12 schools, pre-schools, tertiary institutions, school districts, and government departments. If you would like to learn more about EFEI, please visit www.goodschooldesign.com.

Educational Facilities Effectiveness Evaluation of the Cayman Islands' Government Schools
March 2007

MINISTRY OF EDUCATION
TRAINING • EMPLOYMENT
YOUTH • SPORTS & CULTURE

Building *Brighter* Futures

Throughout this book, we have shown healthy and workable patterns for designing schools. We have even named this book, *The Language of School Design*. And so, on its face, "Should We Stop Building Schools?" might seem like a rhetorical question. We won't deny that it is at least a little rhetorical but not unreasonably so—as we hope to demonstrate.

We know that with nearly $30 billion being committed every year to school construction in this country alone, no one would seriously consider the notion that our society would suddenly stop building schools. But look at the question again—it doesn't ask if we should stop building. Only if we should stop building "schools." It is hardly difficult to make the case that society has come a long way from the time school in its present incarnation was first conceived. While the need for a well-educated citizenry has never been greater, the case to deliver that education in an early 20th century model school has never been weaker.

In any other situation, one could argue—well, why not just make school better and more relevant to today's needs? In the end, that is all we are suggesting, but these kinds of changes cannot happen without first discarding our mental model of school. Because the word school is so loaded with meaning for almost all of us, it can, in and of itself, become an obstacle to change. That is why we are encouraging the use of other terminologies—to weaken our ingrained perceptions and open our minds to other possibilities. Those possibilities crystallize when we ask, if not schools, then what? It allows us to look at what we should be building or even if we should build anything at all. We believe that if schools did all the things we would want them to do and if school facilities followed suit, then we would actually be building *Community Learning Centers*.

Of course, a community learning center (CLC) can be a school but not all schools are CLCs. In order to qualify as a CLC (in our eyes at least), it must meet several conditions:

1. The CLC is seen as a resource for the whole community and not only for parents and children.

2. It is located in a place that is easily accessible to people in the surrounding community—to walkers, bicyclists and those arriving by car and bus.

3. It provides a rigorous, interdisciplinary curriculum enriched by the available learning resources within the community.

4. It provides co-curricular and extra-curricular activities for young people as well as career development options for adults.

5. It is a global hub that connects the community via technology to the rest of the world.

6. It is a part of and not separate or isolated from the community in which it belongs and secures itself in ways that are as far removed as possible from the prisons that so many of our schools have become.

7. Its doors open early in the morning and close late at night.

8. It provides a wide range of services and facilities by bringing together a diverse group of public and private stakeholders and by combining various funding mechanisms.

9. It is a model that applies many of the design principles and patterns outlined in this book.

10. It is created by way of an inclusive and collaborative process.

The diagrammatic representation of a Community Learning Center (Figure B-1) was developed while we were planning a CLC on the outskirts of Chicago, IL. It shows how learning is at the heart of the CLC. By reaching out to make neighborhood connections with homes, businesses, the environment and local institutions, a CLC can provide real-world, rigorous learning experiences to its students that traditional schools would be hard-pressed to provide.

Brookside Center in Victoria, Australia is another good example of a CLC. This project is published in DesignShare.com's library of award-winning projects. The following edited Project Narrative submitted by the architect summarizes this particular community's innovative approach to learning and learning environments. It is also a glimpse into what the future might hold for us here in the United States.

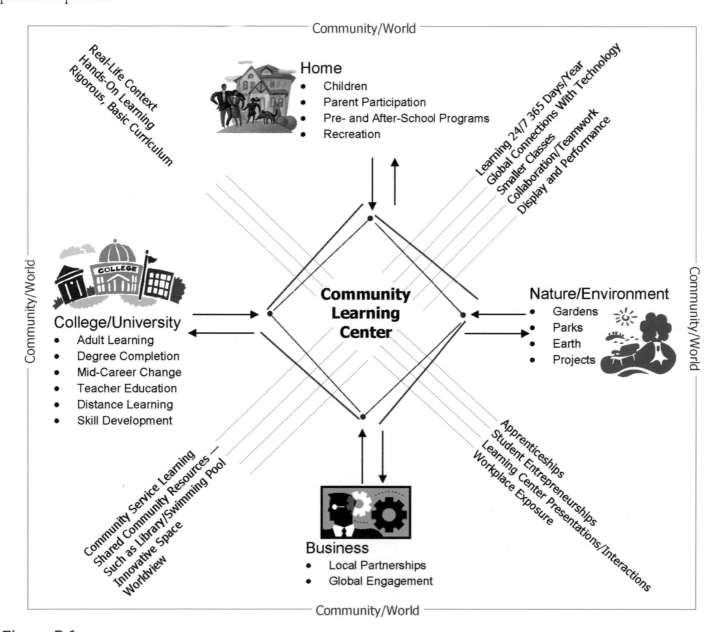

Figure B-1.

Design Principles for a Community Learning Center. ©Fielding Nair International, LLC and Presidential Services Ltd. 2005.

Brookside Center—A CLC in Victoria, Australia

This project involves much more than a conventional school. Its aim is to create a community learning center—a focal point for a "village" of some 3,000 people within a new town that will eventually have a population of 30,000.

There are at least four important ideas expressed in the design, the planning process and the operation of the facilities:

1. Everyone in the new village—especially (but not only) the children—will need to be a lifetime learner. Lifelong education will be an integral part of everyday living.

2. Collaboration and working together in partnerships is a key characteristic of living successfully in the 21st century.

3. Learning is a social process and close interpersonal relations are central to the quality of learning, especially for children.

4. The new information technologies and the library will be the tools with which people access many of their learning opportunities.

Community Learning Center

The idea of a conventional primary school transformed into a community learning center and established as a focal point for village life is well illustrated by the site. The central "Piazza" is a celebration space for the village. It links directly with the school, the neighborhood store, child care facilities, gymnasium, library, IT center, gallery, art room, performance space and staff room/meeting room, all of which are available to the whole community. The result is a learning place for the whole village, especially the children. It is a central and integral part of the village life, just as shopping, recreation, worship, and celebration are integral parts of everyday life.

This is in deliberate contrast to the tradition of withdrawing the school from its community and the community from its school. The idea is to reconnect learning with the everyday life of the village. So instead of keeping people out, the facilities draw people in for purposes that are never far removed from the idea of learning—not only for the children but also for people of all ages.

That some of the learners need safe places and closely supervised places for learning is evident in the design. But the sense of security that comes from the everyday presence of familiar and friendly people is valued here as much as the more physically defensive forms of security provision.

Partnerships

Collaboration and creating new opportunities for enhancing the scope and quality of learning through productive partnerships are of high priority in this project.

In most urban communities in Australia children have a choice between free state schooling and fee paying private (usually religious-based) schooling. This choice is valued by parents and in this community three schools—one state, one Catholic and one nondenominational Christian—have agreed to collaborate to form the village learning center. The result is a very significant enhancement of the range of learning opportunities. Resources are pooled and shared without loss of ownership or identity. Every day the collaborating schools work through the learning process of living harmoniously together despite their differences and their need to compete with each other for students.

Facilities such as a library, the art room, and a fully equipped IT center would simply not be feasible unless sharing occurred. The gymnasium—a joint venture between local government, a sports group and the schools, and the playing fields—a partnership between the community, the schools and a local football club, are two other opportunities that would otherwise not be available at all unless collaboration occurred.

A commitment to collaboration required innovative aspects of the planning process for the learning center. The first step involved the development of the vision with a wide range of stakeholders from the community, local and state government authorities, the developer, education service providers, business, local sporting groups and industry. A small steering committee led by the state education authority and serviced by the developer guided the successful delivery of the vision.

A Sense of Belonging

"Small is preferable" is another idea that has influenced the design and operation of this community learning center. In the past there have been tensions between the apparent advantages of large school size (more specialized facilities, economies of scale, increased prestige, larger staff numbers and bigger budgets) and the advantages of smaller schools (more domestic scale, less alienation and closer interpersonal relationships between students, teachers and parents). A new balance has been struck in this project. Here is a relatively large facility that operates as several relatively small units. Each unit has its own

1. Village Square, store, classrooms above
2. Early childhood and preschool
3. Shared Recreation Centre, sports grounds
4. Shared Library, IT Centre
5. Shared Art and Performance spaces
6. School 1 (Catholic)
7. School 2 (Non-Denominational)
8. School 3 (State)
9. Leased houses as classrooms

Figure B-2.
Brookside Community Learning Centre, Caroline Springs, Victoria, Australia. Architect: Delfin Led Lease. (Photo Courtesy of Gary Blake of Skyworks.)

spaces (along with a number of shared facilities), its own identity (plus occasions when the individual units come together), its own Home Base rooms with Home Base teachers and all the benefits of being small balanced by the opportunities that only come from being large. From a design point of view the commitment to giving every child a "home" place has meant that buildings are dispersed rather than stacked into a large multistoried building.

The emphasis on the idea of "home" has led to an unusual outcome. In order to accommodate a short-term peak in enrollments a group of houses on the periphery of the school site has been specially designed and constructed by a private investor and leased to one of the schools for "home" based accommodation. They will revert to residential uses when the need has passed. This is a further expression of the idea of reconnecting school and community. There is general agreement on campus that this example of flexibility in planning is a better solution than the conventional response of costly and often unsightly "temporary" transportable buildings.

Library

Special mention of the library and IT center is warranted in this overview of the ideas that have influenced this project. Two main considerations have guided the design, location and functions of these elements of the Learning Center.

The library is the point of access to learning for the community from early in the morning to late at night. It operates on weekends and through the normal vacation periods of the schools. Here learners of all ages retrieve information, process it to create data and publish their new knowledge via multi-media technologies.

While every home and workplace in this community is expected to be a relatively high user of the new information and communication technologies, there will always be new,

faster, more powerful and relatively expensive machines that are beyond the reach of many home users. Given that the new technologies are expected to be central to the successful operation of a learning community in which learning can occur any place, any time and at any pace, the IT center, where learners will have access to the latest technologies, will be a vital element. It has been located next to the library and right on the edge of the public "piazza." Here children and adults will work side by side with the aid of the new learning technologies—no doubt with some interesting adjustments to the usual roles of teacher and student.

North Central Shared Facility in Regina, Saskatchewan is an exceptional example of a CLC. This project is currently being designed by Fielding Nair International. The following case study summarizes this particular community's innovative approach to learning and learning environments. It is also a glimpse into what the future might hold for us here in the United States.

North Central Shared Facility— A CLC in Regina, Saskatchewan, Canada

The concept for the North Central Shared Facility (NCSF) has been evolving for several years as various stakeholders in the North Central community explore new and better ways to serve the community. Driven by a commitment to continue or expand their investment in the community and a strong desire to work in an integrated fashion, these agencies have been pushing the delivery of services to a higher level. NCSF breaks the mold from a conventional school.

Initially seen as a simple co-location of agencies with Scott Collegiate High School, it evolved first into a shared facility where space could be utilized more efficiently, and then to a fully integrated model where the stakeholders share common goals and work together as a team. See Figure B-3. There are many important ideas expressed in the design and planning process of the shared facility:

Learning Across the Community (LATC)

LATC is a vision for a high school housed within a shared facility in the North Central community of Regina. This model is based on community involvement, project-based learning initiatives, mentorship, career exposure and service learning opportunities for students, as well as an inter-agency, integrated approach to providing the North Central community the resources it needs to grow and prosper.

This model sets out to change the way students are educated by engaging them in real-world learning experiences within their community. LATC promotes a true integration of students and community as each group supports the other in their initiatives. This learning model represents a significant departure from the passive learning model of the past century by moving toward a student-centered, 21st century educational approach. These innovations will steadily move away from a one teacher, one classroom model of teaching and learning, and more towards flexible teaching arrangements, teacher collaboration, interdisciplinary and inquiry-based teaching and learning, and inclusive practices.

Integrated Model

Scott Collegiate High School is integrated throughout the NCSF. Dedicated high school spaces include Learning Studios, seminar rooms, breakout learning areas, project yards, and cubby neighborhoods. The second floor of the NCSF is home to the four Personalized Learning Communities (PLCs) of Scott Collegiate, which each provide presentation forums, small conference rooms, student workstations, and specialized amenities like kitchenettes. During school hours, the students and staff will occupy PLCs and in the evenings,

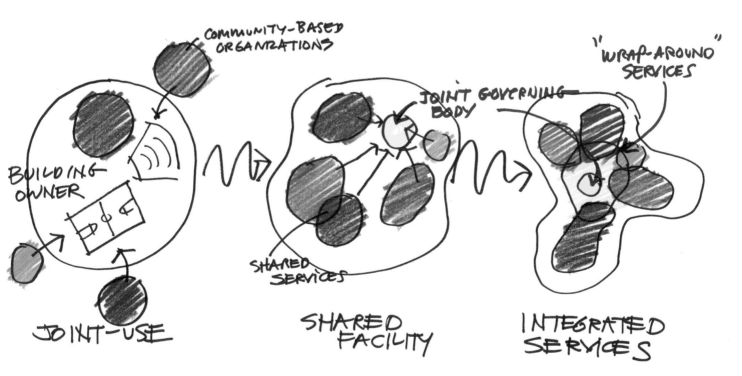

Figure B-3.
The evolution of design patterns for NCSF.

weekends and other times when school is out of session, these spaces become available for booking by Shared Facility partners. NCSF also features a commons space with kiosks, reception desks, group meeting space, lounge areas, café seating, galleries, and student advisories. The Café and the REACH (Regina Education & Action on Child Hunger) Marketplace make healthy food available to the whole North Central community. The Environmental Studio will serve students, community members, and Shared Facility partners as a working greenhouse for studies, of sustainable agriculture, native botany, gardening, foods and nutrition. Students studying horticulture may use this green house studio to establish starter garden plants as part of an effort to encourage fresh food consumption in North Central.

NCSF is designed with particular sensitivity to First Nation and Métis peoples' world views due to their strong presence in North Central Regina. An Elders Area has a large healing room with views to the Central Green. This space is meant for family counseling as well as student mentoring and other Aboriginal teaching activities.

Centres of Excellence

Each of the Shared Facility partners occupies space, categorized into six Centres of Excellence with a specialized focus. The Centres of Excellence are described here:

Centre for Entrepreneurship and Community Development: The Centre serves as a home base for Scott Collegiate Students engaged in the Entrepreneurship and Community Development Program. The North Central Community Association and a variety of programs for recreation and community services are housed here, including REACH and a commercial teaching kitchen. The Centre is located adjacent to both the Elders Area and Central Green to facilitate events.

Regina Public Library and Centre for Information Technology: This Centre of Excellence combines the collections of the high school with the area's branch library. This arrangement will provide students access to a much wider spectrum of resources. This collaboration of shared resources will in turn allow the public library to offer a more varied selection of programs than what is typically offered in a small branch library.

Regina Police Service/Centre for Leadership and Citizenship: Here the Regina Community Police and Probation services are paired. A Community Liaison office is located directly on the new internal commons. The Police Service and Probation Services are combined to provide coordinated services and overlapping support and counseling.

Centre for Fitness, Athletics & Performance Arts: This Centre for Excellence provides fitness and performance art venues for partners. This Centre includes a large gymnasium, fitness studio, multiuse dance and music studio and a recording studio suite. The Centre's design and equipment promote lifelong habits for wellness and personal fulfillment.

Centre for Health and Sciences: This Centre of Excellence combines the various departments and clinics of the Regina Qu'Appelle Health Region in a new collaborative configuration under one roof. Shared functions such as administration, meeting and teaching space will propel a new level of interdepartmental communication and in turn will enable an enhanced level of service to the community. In addition, a Science Studio will be established on the second floor providing much needed science labs and classroom space. Co-locating also opens up many possibilities for student internships and hands-on experience.

Centre for Child and Family Studies: This Centre of Excellence houses both the Scott Infant and Toddler Centre and the Family Resource Centre. Although both daycare centers are separately operated, they share support areas and play spaces. A viewing gallery to the Family Resource Centre serves as a teaching space for both high school and adult programs.

Open Heart, Active Edges

The qualities of permeability, active street edges, pedestrian-friendly scale, and safe, visually supervised spaces are design principles for NCSF (Figure B-4). The shared facility is intended to connect the community and inspire growth and revitalization. Research on safe, healthy urban communities reveals that a key principle in operation is "eyes on the street"—people taking ownership in a neighborhood and watching what goes on. Major spaces in NCSF have direct visual connection to the neighborhood and provide active street edges that invite community. The implication is that the building and the activities and services inside are connected to, and embracing, the community as a whole. See Figure B-5.

Representing the Medicine Wheel, the Central Green is the "heart" of the NCSF. This marquee feature orients and provides "way-finding" to all users while offering a continuous connection to the natural world. Sustainable site features include a drought-resistant landscape with indigenous species, storm water retention, porous paving systems, cisterns, recycled site water to irrigate the other areas of the landscape, wind power generators, and patio pavers of recycled rubber. See Figure B-6.

Figure B-4.
View west along 7th Ave, showing the main south entry to NCSF.

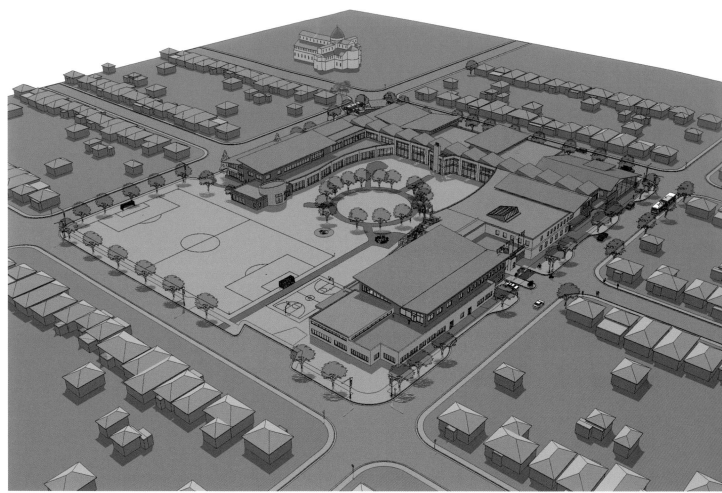

Figure B-5.
View of the Shared Facility campus from the northeast.

The Improved Outcomes

At the core of this endeavor is the belief that the community can create the ideal conditions for learning, which will lead to increased student achievement and that graduates will be prepared for the challenges of career and citizenry in the 21st century. This facility is about helping each student do well in school, supporting each family to lead healthier lives, and providing increased opportunities for each community resident to take part in community life. It's not just a building. This initiative is a unique opportunity to model collaboration, apply it in a very practical way, contribute to the revitalization of an inner

city neighborhood, and enable "Learning Across the Community".

We'll make you a deal. Follow the Brookside Center and North Central Shared Facility models and build a center of learning in partnership with various community establishments. Make it a place that celebrates lifelong learning. Make the center flexible enough to accommodate more or less students as needs change. Make it so kids and adults have access to a wide range of learning resources but can still feel like they belong to a small, caring learning community. Make it safe, but in a way that doesn't feel prison-like. Connect it through technology with the rest

Figure B-6.
View of the Central Green.

of the world and prepare all learners for the new global society they will inherit. If you do all these things, we don't mind if you call it school. And, yes, we will retract the question, *Should We Stop Building Schools* and replace it with a positive statement, *Let Us Keep Building Schools.*

The ability to be creative is the essential ingredient for success in the 21st century. In the 75th anniversary issue of *Business Week*, devoted to the "Global Innovation Economy," it was noted that the knowledge economy has passed, and creativity is a necessity. This applies to our children and to the process that we use when planning schools.

The good news for adults is that recent studies of the brain—the theory of elasticity in particular—have debunked the myth that our brain cells keep dying and that we continually become less intelligent and less creative. On the contrary, the current wisdom is that when you use your brain, its capacity grows! Engage in more creative activities, and you become more creative.

To illustrate the process that leads to the development of a design pattern, we include several sketches. Drawn by Randy Fielding, these sketches led to Pattern #18, Design

for Multiple Intelligences (Figure 18-1). Patterns begin with ideas—with a mix of thoughts, words and images.

Sketch 1 may be described as a simple version of a "mind map." The phrase "mind map" was coined by Tony Buzan in the late 1960s. Research on how the brain works tells us that we learn best in rich environments that stimulate a variety of senses. "Mind maps" are not only images but words and symbols mixed together—all part of the creative process.

Even if you are not an architect or artist, you can prepare the kind of drawing represented by the "mind map." In Sketch 2, the mind map begins to have a spatial structure. Primitive figures, sight lines, rolling hills and a tree are introduced. There is even a line overhead, suggesting a roof.

Sketch 3 includes the essential elements of the space and activities within it; however, there is no accurate scale. The

Figure C-1.
Sketch 1: A "mind map" about Multiple Intelligences, including a guitar (music smart), birds (nature smart), dancer (fitness smart), a quiet work area (social smart) and woman reading a book (word smart).

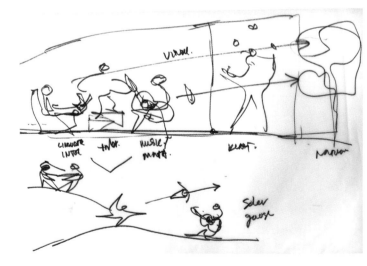

Figure C-2.
Sketch 2: A sketch about spaces and activities that support Multiple Intelligences, including people conversing (interpersonal) and playing a guitar (musical), juggling (kinesthetic) and connecting with rolling hills and a tree (naturalist).

sketch was done quickly, without careful thought about the relative size and position of each of the elements. The figures are too large for the space, reflecting what seemed important while sketching—i.e., the activities, rather than the architecture.

Sketch 4 serves as the black and white "bones" of the final color version of Pattern #18. The accuracy in scale and attention to detail put this drawing in a different category than many of the other patterns. In fact, in addition to being a pattern, this may be considered a particular type of architectural drawing, referred to as a building section and/or an interior elevation. An experienced builder could actually construct a building based on this drawing.

Detailed patterns are not more valuable than diagrammatic patterns. The difference reflects the fact that design is a process, with diagrams and illustrations along the way becoming part of the continuum.

The appropriate level of detail at any point in the process depends on the needs and strengths of the individuals on the planning team. Cruder, more diagrammatic patterns are more open to the imagination, stimulating us at a conceptual level. Broad concepts are often the best place to begin the process, but a detailed pattern can inspire us at a more sensory level.

Ideally, as described in the Introduction, a planning and design process comingles diagrammatic, conceptual ideas with more detailed, concrete ideas. Ideas can be researched by field trips. Sit-down discussions about drawings and design ideas are enhanced by visits to a site and by experiencing the breeze, the sun, the trees and the vistas to the street. These activities will set the stage for the creative process to begin and for the patterns that describe the desired design philosophy and spatial relationships to emerge.

Figure C-3.
Sketch 3: A space for Multiple Intelligences, including a bird feeder under the sloped roof, a juggler, and musician.

Figure C-4.
Sketch 4: The idea in Sketch 1 is developed as an architectural, scaled drawing.

Prakash Nair, REFP
Partner, Fielding Nair International

Prakash Nair is a futurist, visionary planner and President of FNI, one of the world's leading change agents in school design. He is the recipient of several international awards including the prestigious CEFPI MacConnell Award, the top honor worldwide for school design.

Prior to co-founding FNI, Prakash worked for 10 years as Director of Operations for a multi-billion dollar school construction program for New York City.

Prakash serves as a Managing Principal on several projects scattered around the world. He has served as a school planning and design consultant, presenter and/or keynote speaker for clients in Australia (five states), Canada, Cayman Islands, Finland, Great Britain, India, Malaysia, Mexoco, New Zealand, Qatar, Singapore, Thailand, The Netherlands, Spain, the United Arab Emirates, Ukraine and throughout the United States.

By staying current with the research as well as national and international social, economic and cultural trends, Prakash is always able to bring best-practice thinking from many disciplines and fields to bear on education-related problems and projects. This approach has helped education clients save millions of dollars while still achieving or exceeding their schedule and quality expectations.

Prakash's signature talent lies in his ability to communicate his passion for a new approach to education across the globe. He has consistently built strong partnerships with local firms, helped client communities visualize their future, built consensus for uniquely tailored solutions, and helped execute them successfully.

Contact Prakash Nair at Prakash@FieldingNair.com.

Randall Fielding, AIA
Partner, Fielding Nair International

Randall Fielding is the Chairman and Founding Partner of FNI. Randy's achievements have earned him more than a dozen design awards for his work as an architect and planner on high performance projects that foster personalized learning, real-world connections, and small learning communities. He is internationally recognized as an authority on innovative school design and has been selected to serve as a consultant, presenter and/or keynote speaker in Azerbaijan, Australia, Canada, Cayman Islands, Chile, Finland, Germany, Great Britain, India, Portugal, Qatar, Singapore, Sri Lanka, Spain, The Czech Republic, The Netherlands and throughout the United States.

One of Randy's "signatures" is his ability to come down off of the podium, sharing ideas with heads of state, educators, and children with equal passion. This spirit of sharing extends to 2 million people each year, through DesignShare.com, an online forum for innovative learning environments that Randy founded in 1998. He continues to serve as DesignShare's editorial director, but the focus of his work is in helping communities plan and design effective environments for lifelong learning.

Randy inspires though storytelling, shares best practice, and strengthens the skills of other architects to produce the best possible solution within their budget and schedule constraints toward the creation of the most effective environments for lifelong learning.

Contact Randy Fielding at Randy@FieldingNair.com.

Jeffery A. Lackney, PhD, AIA, REFP
Senior Design Architect, Fielding Nair International

Dr. Jeff Lackney committed his entire 20-year practice as a licensed architect to creating high-quality visionary learning environments for children and youth around the world. Jeff was dedicated to authentic community involvement in school planning, believing that the best solutions come from working in concert with people to identify desires and expectations for the future of education, and building on the creative potential of the surrounding community culture.

In addition to his practical experience in school design, Jeff conducted extensive research, published and presented internationally on the influence of the physical setting on learning, assessing the fit between educational programs and older buildings, community-based planning, action research, planning for small learning communities, the role of the physical setting in mediating school climate and culture, post-occupancy evaluation in schools, and neighborhood schools planning. His work has attracted the attention of media outlets CNN.com, *The New York Times*, BBC Radio, National Educational Association (NEA) and *Edutopia*.

Prior to joining FNI, Jeff was assistant professor within the Department of Engineering Professional Development at the University of Wisconsin-Madison where he conducted continuing education courses in architecture and facility management.

Prakash Nair, REFP

Randall Fielding, AIA

Jeffery A. Lackney, PhD, AIA, REFP

Endorsements & Sponsors

THE LANGUAGE OF SCHOOL DESIGN: DESIGN PATTERNS FOR 21ST CENTURY SCHOOLS

This book has been endorsed by:

- The National Clearinghouse for Educational Facilities, at the National Institute of Building Sciences, U.S. Department of Education
- KnowledgeWorks Foundation

References

Alexander, Christopher (1976). *A Pattern Language. Towns, Buildings, Construction.* Center for Environmental Structure Series.

DesignShare Awards Program. (2000, 2001, 2002, 2003 and 2004.) Designshare.com/awards

Fielding, Randall (2004). *What Can $3.6 Billion Buy? Los Angeles School Construction Has a Choice.* Designshare.com/Research/Fielding/LosAngeles_School_Design.asp

Fielding, Randall (2003). *Providing "ngapartji ngapartji," Introduction and Commentary, the 2003 Awards for Innovative Learning Environments.* Designshare.com/awards/2003/commentary2003.asp

Fielding, Randall (2002). *Designing a High School for Collaborative, Project-based Learning.* Designshare.com/Fielding/Harbor_City_International.htm

Fielding, Randall (2000). *Lighting the Learning Environment. An introduction to current issues in lighting as they apply to learning environments.* Designshare.com/Research/Lighting/LightingEnvr1.htm

Gladwell, Malcolm (2000, 2002). *The Tipping Point. How Little Things Can Make a Big Difference.* Little, Brown and Company.

Hoerr, Thomas R. (2000). *Becoming A Multiple Intelligences School.* Association for Supervision and Curriculum Development.

Kohn, Alfie (1999). *The Schools Our Children Deserve—Moving Beyond Traditional Classrooms and "Tougher Standards."* Houghton Mifflin Company.

KnowledgeWorks Foundation (2002). *Dollars and Sense—The Cost Effectiveness of Small Schools.*

Lackney, J.A. (2000). *Thirty-three Educational Design Principles for Schools and Community Learning Centers.* National Institute for Building Sciences (NIBS), National Clearinghouse for Educational Facilities (NCEF), Washington, D.C.

Lackney, J.A. (1999). *Twelve Design Principles for Schools Derived from Brain-Based Learning Research.* Designshare.com/Research/BrainBasedLearn98.htm

Levine, Eliot (2002). *One Kid at a Time. Big Lessons from a Small School.* Teachers College Press.

Lippman, Peter (2004). *The L-Shaped Classroom—A Pattern for Promoting Learning.* Designshare.com/articles/article.asp?article=100

New Schools, Better Neighborhoods (2003). *Case Studies: Joint Use. Minnesota Interdistrict Downtown School.* www.nsbn.org/case/jointuse/minnesota.php

Nair, Prakash (2004). *Building the Future, Lessons from Tasmania.* Education Week, Vol. 23, number 21, page 30, 33.

Nair, Prakash (2003). *30 Strategies for Education Reform.* Designshare.com/articles/article.asp?article=116

Nair, Prakash (2002). *Making Peace with Campfires. Confessions of a Reformed Radical.* Education Week, Vol. 22, number 28, Page 29

Nair, Prakash (2002). *But Are They Learning?* Education Week, Vol. 21, number 29, page 60, 42, 43.

Senge, P.M. (1990). *The Fifth Discipline. The Art and Practice of the Learning Organization.* Random House.

Thornburg, David (Various). *Campfires in Cyberspace* and other publications at The Thornburg Center. www.tcpd.org.